'TRVE': The Norwegian Black Metal Scene: A Subcultural Study of Transgression through Music.

Contents

Trve: The Norwegian Black Metal Scene: A Subcultural study of Transgression through Music.

Chapter 0. Introduction

During the early 90's a small music scene in Norway achieved legendary status through the frequency of murders, church burnings, and a surge of extreme right-wing political apologists arose among other transgressions which occurred in its name. This thesis contains a sub-cultural study which aims to analyse miscellany of the scene and propose answers to questions such as; why this was allowed to happen? What drove the scene members to commit such acts? Did Satanic Black Metal constitute a vehicle for misanthropic activity? (This was the general consensus at the time) Or were the root causes far more overtly complex. Throughout this paper, I hope to offer new investigative perspectives into a youth subculture that due to its uniqueness offers subcultural features that remain unheard of anywhere else.[1]

Throughout history, there are numerous allusions to the rousing effect that music can have on its listeners.[2] From the drums that heralded ancient upcoming war, to the bagpipes that accompany Gaelic soldiers as they march into battle.[3] Quite often, music is the key cultural export of nations, and can be clarified as a language all of its own. For example, "Bhangra," the Punjabi-Sikh form of folk music, now more commonly associated with dance. Lingually while we may be blissfully unaware of meaning or symbolism; the components that form the music speak for themselves in a way that is entirely universal. It can be argued that music can be a form of entertainment or a tool for practical uses upon which the best or worst qualities of humanity can be grown from. The Norwegian Black Metal Scene managed to encapsulate the evil necessary for certain members to thrive while also allowing others to combine their love of Heavy Metal and create something that captures the imagination, and in many cases is incredibly reminiscent of the environment that the artists knew.

I will attempt to answer the following questions in this paper;

1. What is "Black Metal?" Why did the youth of Norway create a sound that was so subversive and remained demonised, even by today's standards of sonic extremity?
2. What were the transgressions committed by the group and what, if any, was the rationale behind them?
3. Where did the political discourse that seemed to underpin "Black Metal" derive from?
4. How was the Norwegian Black Metal Subculture constructed and maintained?

In order to best offer an answer to these questions the paper will be split thus;

Chapter I will contain histories of Black Metal as a genre, post-war Norway and some of the necessary themes that will constitute the rest of this piece of work. In doing so, I intend to offer the reader the appropriate foundations of knowledge to build upon and therefore make dissection of the Black Metaller's world simpler. I will also introduce you to some of the protagonists/antagonists

---

[1] Von Billerbeck, L. L., Nordhausen, F., (2001) *Satanskinder, Der Mordfall von Sondershausen und die rechte Szene*. 3. revised edition, Berlin

[2] Chanan, M. (1994) *Musica Practica: The Social Practice of Western Music from Gregorian Chant to Postmodernism,* London: Verso

[3] Cloonan, M. (2002) 'Killing Me Softly With His Song: An Initial Investigation into the Use of Popular Music as a Tool of Oppression', *Popular Music,* 21 (1): 27-40.

of the Subculture. This knowledge is important as information covering this topic is generally difficult to understand when exposed to it for the first time, and a lot of conceptual ideas fall outside of general criminological understanding, such as "Black Metal" itself and the concept of "Satanism" that became an important contributing factor to the emerging scene.

In chapter II, we will turn our focus in on the Scene itself, how it functioned, its structure and the internal politics that shaped the groups existence. Here the underground phenomenon will also be assessed as to its subcultural template, models of subculture, gang behaviour and neo-tribalism will be utilised in order to correctly define the Norwegian Black Metal Scene on a sociological level. It may be that the Norwegian Black Metal Scene fits comfortably into one category, or redefines boundaries and overlaps two or more societal models. Here we will also look further into the right-wing politics that categorised the scene, and evaluate to what extent the neo-Nazi-esque political discourse dominated the scene, if at all.

Chapter III will take the transgressive acts themselves and analyse in more detail, along with the social context that surrounds each one and what happened in the direct aftermath of each event. Although in this paper I will be attempting to, to an extent, disassociate the musical output from the criminal activities, we will see that the criminality contributed in major ways to the growth and people's awareness of the Scene. Here I will endeavour to explain the satanic surface of the subculture and how this leads into events such as the arson attacks on numerous church buildings.

Chapter IV will deal with the after-effects of the transgressions, and the demise of the second wave of Black Metal. Here we shall discuss why the Norwegian Subculture was so ephemeral, but also identifying the features that have survived and maintained, so that although now there is less coverage of the Scene, Norway still has a reputation for exporting the most popular Black Metal, while other countries such as the US, the UK, France and Eastern European territories are beginning to spawn adequate scenes of their own. I will also argue that although the Norse Scene is dead, Black Metal is healthier now than it ever has been on an international scale.

The final chapter will be a general conclusion, in which I will take all that I have gathered and finalise my theories on the Black Metal subculture, and answer to what extent the negative press surrounding the subculture was entirely accurate or did the actions of a few overshadow the productivity of many more whose names never received a similar notoriety or fame and yet were conduits in which the Black Metal message and musical format took shape.

Trve: The Norwegian Black Metal Scene: A Subcultural study of Transgression through Music.

Fig. 1, Mayhem, circa 1991: (l-r) Hellhammer, Dead, Euronymous, Necro Butcher.[4]

Chapter I. Norwegian Black Metal: a conceptual clarification; an Introduction to the Satanic Metal Underground

For the purpose of this paper my focus will be on the Black Metal scene in Norway of the early 90's, the so-called "second wave of Black Metal"[5] and the subculture that spurned forth in its wake. In researching this group, I will be attempting to add academic understanding to a group that until now is overshadowed by the infamy of the activities within. The Scene itself is far more famous for the notorious "Black Metal Murders"[6] than for its musical output. Currently, the Scene is tarnished and quickly dismissed as anarchic, violent and juvenile. Given the nature of the worldwide press that it received and the relatively obscure and adversarial nature of the sonic templates that were distributed, it's not entirely surprising.

This opening chapter will be a conceptual clarification of Black Metal as a genre of music and a subculture, and it will introduce some of the concepts that I will be working with in an effort to rationalise the irrational, so to speak. It will also offer a brief history of post-war Norway with a focus on the political machinations and model of governance that has remained fairly stable for generations.

The transgressions themselves were committed by a small group, who set out specifically to be as abhorrent as possible; they only served to fuel the fire of infamy and tabloid exposure. It is extremely doubtful that this was their initial intent, some members have become tabloid figures; incredibly adept at manipulating the media. Nevertheless, it is important that we are fully aware of the milieu that the Norwegian youth forced upon their environment and the disruption they caused, but also what happened to them to begin this musical/cultural revolution.

The "Black Metal Murders" is a blanket term that encapsulates the transgressive acts caused by a group of teenagers in Oslo and surrounding areas in the early '90's. The acts we shall look at, (in

---

[4] All images reproduced with permission from Aites, A. & Ewell, A.

[5] Kahn-Harris, K., (2003), "The Aesthetics of Hate Music," *Institute of Jewish Policy Research,* [online] Available at: http://www.axt.org.uk/HateMusic/KahnHarris.htm

[6] Dome, M., (2007), *Murder Music: Black Metal* [online] Available at: http://www.rockworld.tv/MurderMusicPlayer.html

brief) are: the suicide of 'Mayhem's' (arguably, the most notorious Black Metal band) vocalist 'Dead' in 1991, and the subsequent events that took place; the murder of Magne Andreassen, a homosexual, by Bard G. Eithun (aka 'Faust,' ex-drummer with 'Emperor,') in 1992; and the murder of scene leader Oystein Aarseth (aka 'Euronymous' ex-guitarist with 'Mayhem') by his rival, Varg Vikernes (aka 'Count Grisnackh,' ex-bass guitarist of 'Mayhem,' now of 'Burzum') in 1993. We will also analyse the church arson attacks of which, at the height of the Subculture's lifespan (between the years 1992 and 1996) over 50 were raised to the ground and the crimes attributed to members of the scene. This exhaustive list of events has been met with various attempts at reasoning and rationale, and in many cases hypothetical explanations can be diametrically opposed (Von Billerbeck, Nordhausen: 2001).

Black Metal itself first found prominence in Northern England as an extreme subgenre of the (at that time) relatively popular genre of music, Heavy Metal. The band that was arguably responsible hailed from Newcastle-Upon-Tyne, and dubbed themselves 'Venom'. The original trio coined the term "Black Metal" as the title of their second album released in 1982.[7] An early example of the sonic extremity that would follow; the high-treble guitar tone was present, and lyrics that dealt with Satan. Satanism also became a focal point on certain songs, on others the lyrical focus shifted no further than other bands who celebrated "rock n' roll" amongst other aspects of the "heavy metal lifestyle." In essence, the tone was that of tongue-in-cheek humour and the trio were fully aware of their incompetence with their instruments. Without the insider-knowledge gained from being a scene member at the time, it could have been taken in a very authentic light. The ludicrous nature of their promotional photographs: liberal amounts of skulls, all members dressed in leather, spikes and "bullet belts" (which are precisely what the name suggests; leather belts adorned with bullet casings) seemed to suggest to a media that casually covered such bands (for reasons of voyeurism and ridicule more than anything else) that this was evil. This band stood at the forefront of a codified evil that casual listeners in 1982 would be genuinely scared of, believing in the throwaway comments the band made that their music invoked demonic presence etc. Similar bands appeared in Scandinavia such as Hellhammer (the band that would later become Celtic Frost), Mercyful Fate and Bathory, who were the first bands to actually contain Satanists to create Black Metal. Throughout the 80's due to this first wave of bands, the Black Metal sound became a blueprint: Treble-heavy distorted guitar tones, blast beat drumming (blast beat: a repeated sixteenth-note figure, played at a high tempo) and screamed or shouted vocals through an incredibly low fidelity production.[8]

As Black Metal spread across Northern Europe, the youth of Norway, (specifically, white, middle-class, socially-included males) picked up on this new phenomenon, and took it as their own, combining the existing template with "Viking Bloodlust"[9] such as the addition of references to Old Norse literature in the lyrics.[10] The bands who gradually began forming felt more familiarity with the idea of Black Metal, as it deviated from the existing punk element, (of which there was a quite healthy scene in Norway: 'Drunk,' 'Within Range' (whose lead vocalist 'Messiah' was originally a member of Mayhem) and 'Siste Dagers Helvete,' to name but three), at the time the Norwegian

---

[7] Black Metal, (1982), Neat

[8] Kalis, Q., (2004) *Black Metal: A brief guide,* [online] Available at:
http://www.chroniclesofchaos.com/Articles/rants/6-668_black_metal_a_brief_guide.aspx

[9] Steinke, D., (1996), "Satan's Cheerleaders," *SPIN Magazine,* February, pg.62-71

[10] Von Helden, I., (2011), "'A Forure Normannorum, Libera Nos Domine!' *A Short History of Going Berserk in Scandinavian Literature & Heavy Metal,*" *Can I Play With Madness?,* Oxford: Inter-Disciplinary Press

punk musicians dealt primarily with US-centric politics[11] and Euronymous felt that the Norwegian youth were disconnected from international policy, and wanted to avoid "social issues" and sing about "death, black and darkness."[12] Although Euronymous was a member of the most left-wing communist party in Norway, he didn't believe that political machinations should ever form a part of Mayhem.

To date, all the surviving Norwegian Black Metal Scene members cite 'Venom' as an early influence. However, due to the lack of context or naivety on the Norwegian youth's part, nearly all of them misinterpreted the tongue-in-cheek quality of the early recordings. The second wave of Black Metal had been transformed into a new shape; new meaning had been transplanted to it. The faux-Satanism inherent in Venom's efforts had been subverted. Without the proper teachings or tenets, the youth didn't realise their brand of Satanism was so far removed from the foundations of Anton LaVey's "Church of Satanism" i.e., LaVey himself ridiculed the Norwegian Scene and until his death, refused to acknowledge "Heavy Metal" or any of its derivatives, as music. The Norwegian's Satanism was uncomplicated and anarchic. If the Christian Bible celebrated and commended an action, they would condemn it and perform antonymous acts. For example, Genesis 38: 8-10 can be interpreted as a condemnation of masturbation. Upon reading and interpreting in this way, Aarseth would frequently masturbate outside in the forests around Oslo. As bands formed across Oslo that shared this Black Metal vision of mutated theistic Satanism, a close-knit scene emerged which circulated around Euronymous' record shop "Helvete" (meaning: Hell), the shop acted as an expansion of his record label "Deathlike Silence Productions."

Norwegian Black Metal has always held a certain appreciation for nature innate in its lyricisms and style, a component that stems from the almost mythical scenery that the country is noted for.[13] The natural world is seen as not just a literal portrayal of the pride that the musicians had for their landscape, but a metaphor for the mutual sense of primitive atavism for the long-gone days when mankind existed in a more bestial state. Although the paradigm has shifted since the "glory days" of the Norwegian Scene, the respect for nature has been added to the mix of a number of newer Black Metal bands such as: 'Abigail Williams,' 'Wolves In The Throne Room,' 'Alcest' and 'Negura Bunget.'

Norway in the early 1990's: a Socio-Political Retrospective and Brief History

It is imperative that we attempt to understand Norway on a socio-political level before moving onwards towards analysing the youth subculture explosion of the 1990's. In the following passages, I will first begin by delving into the history and political structure of Norway, as both disciplines are pivotal in comprehending the Norwegian culture.

Norway is a fairly young country, having only declared independence from Sweden in 1905. As with the majority of Europe, the Norsemen were of Pagan beliefs, with Christianity being introduced and gradually enveloping and replacing Paganism as the religion of the masses between the 8th and 12th Centuries. Although King Olav Tryggvason (960s'-1000 AD) officially adopted Christianity in 994 AD;[14] the Norsemen's pride in their paganism meant that they were reticent in adapting to the new

---

[11] Frobenius, N., (2004), *Treori Og Praksis,* (meaning: "Theory and Practice"), Oslo: Gyldendal
[12] Kristiansen, J., (2011), "Metalion: The Slayer Mag. Diaries" New York: Bazillion Points
[13] Negarestani, R., "Melancology," *Black Metal Symposium III*, A Lecture, 13th January 2011
[14] Larsen, K., (1948) *A History of Norway,* Princeton: Princeton University Press

religion. Their stubbornness would lead to King Olav converting Pagan "heathens" by force/torture[15] and in some cases, with fatal results.[16] As of January 1st 2010, 79.2%[17] of Norwegians are believed to be aligned to Protestantism (which throughout the Northern European territories, is known as 'Lutheran Catholicism'). This represents a drop from previous figures.[18] The strength of their belief is disputable as if a citizen is born Norway to one or more Norwegian parents, they are automatically added to list of Lutheran Catholics, and if they wish to renounce this faith (or if they never had it in the first place) they must actively "sign out" of the Church. In the 2005 'Eurobarometer' poll only 32% of Norwegians admit to believing in a God,[19] and currently only 12% regularly attend religious ceremonies.

The structure of the Norwegian Government is a constitutional monarchy. This Governmental structure provides an early clue to the Black Metal Subculture's exhibitions of Satanism. In addition to maintaining their monarchy, which as of January 1991 has been headed by King Harald V, the country has a single supreme Parliamentary House; the Storting. It is staffed by a fully elected body, based on elections of party lists (not individual members) every four years by proportional representation.[20] Interestingly however, it is a national requirement that 50% of the Storting must comprise of those of Christian denomination, meaning that the Christian Church holds far more legitimate political power over Norway than in other countries.[21]

As a country, Norway has a landmass of 383,759 square kilometres with a population of little over 4.9 million,[22] making it the second least densely populated country in Europe.[23] Economically, Norway's main export is oil and various fuel products; this revenue contributes around $40 billion (£21 billion) per annum to the nation's GDP (BBC NEWS: Norway Country Profile). The Sovereign Wealth Fund dubbed "Government Pension Fund" into which this money is placed is currently valued at $571.5 billion,[24] (which is the second highest in the world, behind UAE's "Abu Dhabi Investment Authority" at £627 billion). Consequently, from a state welfare point of view, Norway has a fantastic record of welfare co-ordination for its nationals. In studying Esping-Andersen's work on models of welfare state,[25] we can see the socio-democratic "Nordic model" operates thus; the state

---

[15] Boyesen, H. H., Keary, C. F., (1900), *A History Of Norway: From The Earliest Times,* Whitefish: Kessinger Publishing, LLC

[16] Longfellow, H. W., (1863), "The Saga of King of Olaf," *Tales of a Wayside Inn: Part First, The Musician's Tale.* [online] Available at: http://www.gutenberg.org/ebooks/25153

[17] Den Norske Kirke, *Medlemskap i Den norske kirke* (meaning: Membership of the church of Norway) [online] Available at: http://www.kirken.no/index.cfm?event=doLink&famId=230

[18] Soucy, D. & Volkmar, M, (2006), *True Mayhem in Norway,* [online] Available at: http://www.nmchs.com/activities/talon/tal06nov/p07novtal.pdf

[19] Eurobarometer, (2005) "Social Values, Science and Technology," *Eurobarometer,* Brussels: European Commission [online] Available at: http://ec.europa.eu/public_opinion/archives/ebs/ebs_225_report_en.pdf

[20] Rokken, S., Valen, H., (1962), "The Mobilization of the Periphery: Data on Turnout, Party Membership and Candidate Recruitment in Norway," *Acta Sociologica,* Vol. 6, 1, 111-152.

[21] Stortinget, *Constitution- Complete Text,* [online] Available at: http://www.stortinget.no/en/In-English/About-the-Storting/The-Constitution/The-Constitution/

[22] BBC News, *Norway Country Profile* [online] Available at: http://news.bbc.co.uk/1/hi/world/europe/country_profiles/1023276.stm

[23] *Statistics Norway,* [online] Available at: http://www.ssb.no/english/subjects/02/befolkning_en/

[24] SWF Institute, *Sovereign Wealth Fund Rankings: Largest Sovereign Wealth Funds by Assets Under Management,* [online] Available at: http://www.swfinstitute.org/fund-rankings/

[25] Esping-Andersen, G., (1999). *Social Foundations of Postindustrial Economies.* Oxford: Oxford University Press.

distributes funds to both services such as healthcare and education, and also to individuals as benefits, with the minimum of bureaucratic intervention. Benefits are distributed based on fulfilment of categories that the claimant adheres to. These are incredibly simple to understand, resulting in over half the population claiming benefits as a main contributor to their annual income.[26] The strength of the Nordic welfare state has been such that while other notable welfare states have fallen under scrutiny and savage mutilation, i.e. the United Kingdom, Norway's has recovered time and time again and proved highly resilient.[27]

During the Second World War, the fascist politician Vidkun Quisling seized control of Norway in a Nazi-backed coup d'etat, and ruled from 1942-1945. The Quisling regime contained ministers from his party the 'Nasjonal Samling' (meaning: National Gathering) and were an active participant in the Nazi's Final Solution.[28] After the war, Quisling was put on trial and found guilty of charges of embezzlement, high treason and murder; he was subsequently executed in October 1945.[29] In the wake of Quisling's actions, Scandinavian countries were less than eager to place such a right-leaning party in democratic opposition in the Storting. Consequently, right-wing parties were demonised and banned from legitimate political representation. As we shall observe, this is a dangerous method as when driven underground, political groups do not receive a democratic voice and avoid the scrutiny of official political parties; resulting in frustration with potentially devastating consequences.

This intrinsic mistrust in right-wing ideals lead to The Norwegian Labour Party riding on a wave of confidence into the 1990's as they enjoyed a fairly consistent majority (see: Appendix. I), the elected Prime Minister Gro Harlem Brundtland, a notable environmental activist held her period in office with an immense degree of popularity. At this time nearly all parties in Norway were between left-wing and centrist, right-wing interests were served largely by the Conservative Party, following the still-smouldering phantom of Quisling and his legacy.[30] Brundtland's Government possessed a relaxed attitude to immigration, compared to the Immigration ban imposed in 1975,[31] (this allowed family members, students, experts and refugees/asylum seekers access)[32] which resulted in the introduction of new races and cultures to a country in which the population had been overwhelmingly "Norse."

 The new arrivals amassed a significant opposition to the perceived cultural norms within the country, and inevitably a backlash occurred. In the minds of the youth, who had already been indoctrinated into believing that the paganism of their ancestors had been forcibly removed, this introduction of new cultures arrived hand in hand with what they saw as the failure of the socio-democratic system and the Christian political power that guides it.

---

[26] Eriksen, T. H., (2006), "We Have Everything But That's All We Have: Outsourcing the Welfare State," *Verkstad* vol. 6, [online] Available at: http://folk.uio.no/geirthe/Outsourcing.html

[27] Huber, E., Stephens, J.D., (2001), *Development & Crisis of the Welfare State: Parties & Policies in Global Markets,* Princeton: Princeton University Press

[28] Dahl, H. F., (1999), *Quisling: A Study in Treachery.* Stanton-Ife, A. M., (trans.). Cambridge: Cambridge University Press

[29] Hayes, P. M., (1971), *Quisling: the career and political ideas of Vidkun Quisling, 1887–1945,* David & Charles: United Kingdom

[30] Arter, D., (1999), *Scandinavian Politics Today,* Manchester: Manchester University Press.

[31] Gullestad, M., (2002), "Invisible fences, Egalitarianism, Nationalism and Racism," *J. Roy. anthrop. Inst.,* 8, pp. 45-63

[32] It is a legal requirement that immigrants to Norway undertake 250 hours of lessons on communicating in Norwegian.

If we transplant these connotations into a social context, the influence of the church would become an authoritarian figure over those citizens who didn't even believe in its dogma, and felt like it was being "shoved down their throats."[33] This is not only a source of discomfort for non-believers but also to those who are aware that when Christianity arrived in Scandinavia, the results were the displacement of the pagan ideals and Gods that they took great pride in. This disenchantment with a culture that had banished their own could be argued as a root cause of the anti-Christian sentiment and the church burnings.[34] In addition to the political right who believed vehemently in resisting immigration (Norway did not sign the Schengen Agreement until 1996, implementing it in 2001) were being soundly ignored and dismissed. This dissatisfaction with the left-leaning Government combined with the absence of any established political party[35] representing the right-wing, produced a rightwards shift in the political machinations of the Black Metal Scene. Suddenly, where before lay a white majority with proud national heritage but for the most part- inactive; a new (although constantly present) wave of racist and anti-immigration views surged forth from the peaceful suburbs of Norway (Taylor: 2010).

Although it has been argued by Kahn-Harris among others,[36] that the political implications of the right-wing shift have been overstated and that the political machinations of the youths were too under-developed to be recognised as legitimate and they were simply aligning themselves with a group. As Kristian Eivind Espedal (aka 'Gaahl' ex-vocalist with 'Gorgoroth') has stated in a 2008 magazine interview:

> *"In the early '90s, there were all these different youth gangs in Norway and one thing led to another. I was involved in gang fights and had false friends … There was no political disposition – not with me nor any of my friends. But you had to profess allegiance to a certain group if you wanted to defend yourself and not get your ass kicked."*[37]

This admission from a member with significant cultural capital, can be accepted as a valid viewpoint among certain scene members, and also suggests that some were indoctrinated upon taking part in what Gaahl considered "gangs." His indoctrination into racist right-wing ideals came to the fore in the Polish Holocaust, 1995 interview, when he stated support for Adolf Hitler and Varg Vikernes among others. He also voiced a dislike of "niggers", "mulattoes" (people of mixed race) and Muslims calling them "subhuman." (Polish Holocaust: 1995) With hindsight we can observe the youthful naivety that caused the then-21 year-old Gaahl to commit such unfounded hatred to print, but at the time there was a very real fear that there was a brooding political unrest and a descent into extremism.

---

[33] *"Polish Holocaust"* Magazine, (1995) "Interview with Gaahl" Available at:
http://i355.photobucket.com/albums/r455/WD37/76ec8a07.jpg
[34] Kahn-Harris, K., (2004), "The "Failure" of Youth Culture: Reflexivity, Music & Politics in the Black Metal Scene," *European Journal of Cultural Studies,* 7 (1), pp. 95-111. [online] Available at: http://eprints.gold.ac.uk/2196/
[35] Taylor, L. W., (2010), "Nordic Nationalisms: Black Metal takes Norway's Everyday Racism to the Extreme" *The Metal Void: the First Gatherings,* Oxford: Inter-Disciplinary Press
[36] Kahn-Harris, K., (2007), Extreme Metal: Music and Culture on the Edge" London: Berg
[37] Kunhemund, G., (2008), "GORGOROTH Frontman Opens Up About His Sexual Orientation: 'I've Never Made Any Secret About It' - Oct. 29, 2008" *RockHard (Ger.) via Blabbermouth.net.* [online] Available at: http://www.roadrunnerrecords.com/blabbermouth.net/news.aspx?mode=Article&newsitemID=107859

Now we have a vague idea of the history of Black Metal, from its humble roots in the North of England, the post-war History of Norway, and the structure of their Governmental system dubbed the "Nordic Model." With these in mind, as well as a short introduction to some of the individuals who will be subjects in this paper, it is essential to treat this chapter as the building blocks on which the remainder of the paper will rest upon. This understanding is the key to this much maligned musical youth subculture. The next chapter will begin to construct on top of the building blocks as we look inwards towards the subculture and begin to hypothesise on scene structure, diversification, membership and the method behind the "madness."

Trve: The Norwegian Black Metal Scene: A Subcultural study of Transgression through Music.

fig.2, Leif Gylve Nagell "Fenriz," drummer and vocalist with Darkthrone, circa 1992.

Chapter II: The Norwegian Black Metal Inner Circle, scene politics and the infra-structure of the subculture

The aim of this chapter is three fold; we will observe the fallacy of the notorious "Black Metal Inner Circle" through the eyes of those that were a part of the scene, and the collective evidence against its existence. We will also seek out the truth behind the rightwards shift that characterises the Scene, and finally test the Norwegian Black Metal subculture against recognised models of subcultural theory to investigate its functionality.

The Black Metal Inner Circle and the perceived rightwards shift

If one is to look at the Norwegian Black Metal subculture merely through the lens of media exposure, the picture consists of a tight group of bloodthirsty, organised criminals dedicated to evil and pursuing a war on the powers-that-be. Although Euronymous liked to maintain this illusion of a "Black Metal Inner Circle," other scene members notably Vikernes debunk this myth as another example of Aarseth's manipulation tactics. Whereas, realistically, the picture emerges of a loosely-knit group of teenagers, who liked to play the same sort of music and generally find their own image,[38] much in the same way that youth cultural movements have always done; "Mods," "Rockers," "Goths," "Emos" and countless other examples, forming a microcosmic social circle. Leif Gylve Nagell (aka 'Fenriz' drummer with 'Darkthrone'), is a notable scene leader who, by his own admission, stayed apolitical and offers an unbiased view of the events that shaped the Black Metal scene.[39] Fenriz retained his focus on music; both that of his multiple projects and the scores of underground bands he supports. Vikernes has said of him that he has: "very specific goals and it is difficult to know what he wants." (Aites, Ewell: 2009). If there was a case for the tight group of bloodthirsty

---

[38] Myers, B., (2009), "Don't blame black metal for Varg Vikernes' extremism," The Guardian, [online] Available at: http://www.guardian.co.uk/music/musicblog/2009/mar/12/varg-vikernes-grishnackh-black-metal?INTCMP=SRCH

[39] Aites, A., Ewell, A., (2009), *Until The Light Takes Us,*

organised criminals, then two of the most prominent scene members would be aware of each others' ambitions. In fact in such a close group, you could be safe to assume they would share the same goals.

Fenriz is angry with the explosion and eventual commercialisation of the black metal scene (Aites, Ewell: 2009). Gaahl shares less disdain about the issue (see next chapter) but declared that at its root Black Metal was "purely self-centred." Contrastingly, we can assume from Aarseth's actions in manipulating the media following Dead's suicide and generally working to gain exposure, his attitude eventually began to diverge from the shared vision (see next chapter). This can be taken as further evidence that the "Black Metal Inner Circle" was fallacious and the result of a comment by Euronymous that the media were only too happy to regurgitate, as it aided the need to understand this cultural phenomenon by introducing the essence of an idea of organised crime. It (wrongly) dispelled the anarchic aspect of the Black Metal Scene, as the general populace will comprehend elements of organisation far clearer than a subculture built around anarchy.

Nagell has commented that the two diverged after Vikernes "introduced his politics to Burzum".[40] In truth, the main concerns of Nagell and doubtless others at the dawn of the 90's was tape-trading[41] internationally, and playing music with friends while donning corpse paint and black clothes (Myers: 2010). The politically minded although over-exposed, were in the minority.[42] If we recall Gaahl's comments from above concerning allegiance to youth gangs over political allegiance, we can surmise that the gang leaders would provide a massive influence over those who exist underneath them. Therefore the politics of these figureheads, many of whom previously meddled in right-wing activities before the Black Metal scene had even been conceived, shone through. For example, Vikernes was originally a member of the youth right-wing skinhead movement that existed in Bergen, toward the latter part of the 80s.[43]

Outsiders looking in at Norway during this period comment on the extremity of the racial hatred committed by the Black Metal Scene, but are usually ignorant to the anti-immigrant culture that has always been innate in Norway.[44] Gullestad puts forward that in Norway the cultural identity of its inhabitants depends of *likhet* (meaning: "similarity") and must be reinforced by others who are seen to possess the same characteristics, the most obvious feature is found in skin-colour. This perceived sameness may be a complete fallacy, but due to the historical isolation from other cultures of Norse people, the implication is that the implied equality exists through memic reproduction (Gullestad: 2002). Historically, paganism has been encouraging of this "sameness." The Aryan tribes that made up the inhabitants of early Scandinavian territories were the ideal human race envisioned by Hitler's

---

[40] Baddeley, G., (2010), *Lucifer Rising: A Book of Sin, Devil Worship & Rock n' Roll,* 3rd edition, Plexus Publishing Ltd.: London.

[41] Tape-trading was a method of distributing bootlegged cassette copies of music through correspondence with others, whether home-recorded copies of albums or demos and rehearsal tapes recorded by the bands themselves. This method has fallen by the wayside after the rise of the internet. However, at this time it was the preferred method for "alternative" music fans to discover new bands and new sounds.

[42] Davisson, J., (2010), "Extreme Politics and Extreme Metal: Strange Bedfellows or Fellow Travellers?" *The Metal Void: The First Gatherings,* Oxford: Inter-Disciplinary Press

[43] Goodricke-Clarke, N., (2002), *Black Sun: Aryan Cults, Esoteric Nazism and the Politics of Identity,* New York: New York University Press

[44] Gullestad, M., (2004), "Blind Slaves of our Prejudices: Debating 'Culture' and 'Race' in Norway," *Ethnos: Journal of Anthropology,* Vol. 69, 2, pp.177-203

Third Reich. Even studying the connection between the early Norwegian paganism and Nazi-controlled Germany uncovers surprising correlations; the notorious "S" that made up the logo for Hitler's secret police force: the "SS" was derived from the "Elder Furthark" (2nd- 8th Century) runic symbol: *"sowlio"* meaning *"sun,"*[45] in translation the title of the rune became *"sig"* by Himmler's occult specialist Karl Maria Willigut[46] and became a symbol for victory.[47] Also, the runic symbol *"algiz"* closely translated to modern English as "z" represents refusal to give up one's heritage when performing the occult art of casting rune stones,[48] thus a perfect symbol for inspiring Nazi Germany and Norwegian Pagans. It is well acknowledged that Hitler used Pagan symbology to inspire his faction to power, and although the Norwegians now consider Quisling as synonymous with "traitor." When considering politics, it is evident that a general xenophobic attitude throughout Scandinavia is silent and seemingly separate from right-wing politics. Whereas when members of the Black Metal Scene such as Vikernes rejoined the elements of xenophobia and right-wing thoughts, there were others that were staunch in their belief that Black Metal should be apolitical, such as Fenriz and Euronymous.

Norwegian Black Metal viewed through Subcultural/Gang/Neo-Tribal theory

As this paper attempts to study the Norwegian Black Metal Scene at a sociological level as well as analysing their transgressions; it is important that we understand the structure of the proponents who created what became known as the "Second Wave of Black Metal." In order to understand the scene on a sociological level, we must try to find an accurate fit for the Norwegian Black Metal Scene among existing models of social groupings. In this part, I will review the literature surrounding gangs, subcultures and neo-tribes to show the divergence and unique nature of the Satanic Metal Underground.

Subcultural Theory

The term "subculture" is used to denote groups with their own culture functioning inside a larger culture/society. Hebdige argued that a subculture is a response to disaffection within a society and helps to bring together like-minded individuals to form an identity and a social network at a more familiar/personal level.[49] Due to the personal features that combine in order to create and align to a subculture, it can be argued that the ties that bind a subculture can be stronger than the cultural ties that bind the entire society (which continues to function concurrently). [50] It has also been said that members of a subculture can not only identify each other's allegiance by their clothes, mannerisms and choice of musical consumption, but also the strength of the other's allegiance.[51] For example, a person who wears a t-shirt with an underground band logo adorned on it; by its nature, an underground band's logo will only be recognisable to a few. This act will gain more respect than someone who wears a t-shirt with a logo from a perceived mainstream artist/band).[52] As previously

---

[45] Page, R.I., (2005), *Runes*, pp. 8, 15, and 16, The British Museum Press.

[46] Hale, C., (2003), *Himmler's Crusade: The Nazi Expedition to Find the Origins of the Aryan Race,* Hoboken, N.J.: John Wiley & Sons,

[47] Please see: http://usminc.org/hitler3.html

[48] Page, R. I. (1999), *An Introduction to English Runes,* Boydell Press,

[49] Hebdige, D., (1979), *Subculture: The Meaning of Style,* New York: Routledge

[50] Yinger, J. M., (1960), "Contraculture and Subculture," *American Sociological Review*, vol.25, 5.

[51] Huq, R., (2006) *'Beyond subculture'* New York: Routledge

[52] Gardner, R. O., (2010), "Introduction: spaces of Musical Interaction: Scenes, subcultures and communities,"

alluded to, members of subcultures will assess each other's allegiance within the scene through their consumption choices; this can be seen as a battle for elitism, as certain members will inevitably strive to possess more "subcultural capital."[53] Those with the subcultural capital, the knowledge which leads to increased status, will rise in the hierarchy of the scene. Furthermore, a subculture can possess normative values that counter or subvert the values of the entire mass culture. For this some subcultures can be met with negative backlash and become "folk devils,"[54] unwittingly feeding the media machine, which highlights any negativity and rightly or wrongly associate it to the subculture. Consequently, a moral panic develops as the subculture becomes a perceived "threat to societal values." In these eventualities, there have been laws passed to legislate against the activities of some subcultures.[55]

However, features of a subculture that initially belonged to the group exclusively, if the style becomes a media interest, can and invariably will, be accepted commercially and mass-marketed[56] in attempts by businesses to capture the essence of what's "in." This process is especially true for music-based subcultures, for which the turn-around between a subculture adopting a certain dress code and that style being commercialised and sold on the high street can be remarkably quick.[57] This somewhat negates the meaning of that particular artefact to the "real" members of the group, and they will either accept this, evolve their subculture in a new way,[58] or react with disdain against those that buy the mass-marketed t-shirts as opposed to the "bedroom-pressed" items.

If we apply the above on to the Norwegian Black Metal Scene, we can observe numerous parallels. The most notable example being the idea of a moral panic, but there has never been an initiative to curtail Black Metal. This may be because of Norway's general attitude towards music. Historically, Norwegian music has always consisted of minor scale-led melody to create "hauntingly atmospheric soundscapes" evoking the natural landscape of the country,[59] in addition to the national pride that has always been a contributing factor of Norwegian composition. Therefore the music that is created by the Black Metallers is quite closely linked to the traditional folk music styles and classical composers, such as the most famous of Norwegian composers Edvard Greig.[60] Over 20% of Norway's population will attend at least one of the many music festivals that occur all over the country. Norway has a very encouraging attitude to music from all genres and the festivals themselves denote highly diverse acts; visitors to this year's Oya! Rock Festival will be able to experience Norwegian Black Metal/punk hybrids: 'Kvelertak' and UK-based indie/folk band 'Noah & The Whale' on the same stage.[61] There are reportedly 550,000 music venues of note scattered around Oslo

---

Studies in Symbolic Interaction, 35. 71-77
[53] Thornton, S., (1995), *Club Cultures: Music, Media, and Subcultural Capital*. Cambridge: Polity Press.
[54] Cohen, S. (1973). *Folk Devils and Moral Panics*, St Albans: Paladin
[55] Hall, S. Jefferson, T., (1993), Resistance through Rituals: Youth Subcultures in Post-War Britain,London: Routledge
[56] Howes, D., (1996), *Cross-cultural consumption: global markets, local realities.* New York: Routledge
[57] Blair, E. M., (1993), "Commercialization of Rap Music Youth *Subculture." Journal of Popular Culture* 27.3 21-33
[58] Goldstein-Gidoni, O., (2003), "Producers of 'Japan' in Israel: *Cultural appropriation* in a non-colonial context." *Ethnos:Journal of Anthropology* 68.3, 365
[59] Cronshaw, A., (2000), "Fjords and Fiddles" *World Music, Vol. 1: Africa, Europe and the Middle East*, pp 211–218. New York: Penguin
[60] Grimley, D., (2006), *Grieg: Music, Landscape and Norwegian Cultural Identity*, Suffolk: Boydell Press
[61] http://oyafestivalen.com/pages/eng/1-news

alone.[62] The socio-democratic system once again comes into play, ensuring that even the most underground musicians are suitably compensated for what would usually be an incredibly low-paying franchise.

It therefore can be argued that the Norwegian Black Metal Scene is a true subculture; unfortunately, there are two flaws which prevent the Scene from being classed as pure. Primarily the issue of acceptable limits of sphere of influence; the first rumblings of the Scene began in Oslo, and those willing to contribute to the scene descended upon Oslo and made contacts with members of 'Mayhem' through Helvete and Deathlike Silence Productions. Varg Vikernes, Olve Eikemo (aka 'Abbath,' multi-instrumentalist with 'Immortal') and Harald Nævdal (aka 'Demonaz,' guitarist with 'Immortal'- previously, all three were members of the band 'Amputation') all originally hailed from Bergen, a city on the other side of Norway. Although at the beginning, there was no geographical limit for who could be considered "TRVE," as time went on, the sphere of acceptability tightened to Oslo and its neighbouring towns, (the furthest band from the centre of Oslo to still be considered one of the original "big four"[63] "TRVE" bands is 'Emperor,' from Notodden, 56 miles away).[64] As a true subculture has no geographical limit, (Huq: 2006) and should be accessible to all, this is a major flaw. Secondly, the commercialisation element that allows for re-interpretation of the subculture's features and styles and subsequent regurgitation (by fashion labels/record companies etc.) is implausible, attributable to the subversive and to an extent- disturbing state that the Scene manifested itself in. So, although Norwegian Black Metal Scene shares many features of subcultural theory, (and in other Black Metal scenes around the world, there may be evidence to retain the subculture label) but in this case, we must search other areas.

"Gang" Theory

Another template which we could try to fit the idea of the Norwegian Black Metal Scene into is that of the gang. A "youth gang" can be at its simplest level be judged by the relative age of its participators and the involvement of such members in transgressive behaviour.[65] Beyond this fairly simple definition there has been much argument as to a more accurate depiction of what constitutes gang participation and behaviour.[66] Thrasher classically surmised that in defining gangs, that finding what it is typical between groups is more advantageous to research than what is unique to each.[67] He formed a list of operational characteristics; he believed that each gang exhibited: a spontaneous and unplanned origin; intimate face to face relation between members; a sense of organization, morale and solidarity that would supersede that of a mob; tendency to assert itself in hostile territory; a shared "common tradition;" and a preference to a certain geographic territory as far as membership and protection are concerned. Thrasher's definition is useful to us in viewing the

---

[62] Furniss, O., (2010), "Oslo: Norway's music and Festival Paradise," *guardian.co.uk,* [online] Available at: http://www.guardian.co.uk/travel/2010/jan/30/oslo-norway-music-festivals-gigs

[63] Referring to the "Big Four" of Black Metal: 'Mayhem,' 'Emperor,' 'Darkthrone,' and 'Immortal.' (Kristiansen: 2011).

[64] http://tinyurl.com/oslo-to-notodden

[65] Howell, J. C., (1998), "Youth Gangs: An Overview," *Juvenile Justice Bulletin*, Washington DC: Office of Juvenile Justice and Delinquency Prevention.

[66] Esbensen, F-A., Winfree, L. T., He, N., Taylor, T. J., (2001), "Youth Gangs and Definitional Issues: When is a gang a gang, and why does it matter?" *Crime & Delinquency*, 47, 105 [online] Available at: http://tinyurl.com/gang-definition

[67] Thrasher, F. M., (1927) The Gang: A Study of 1313 gangs in Chicago, Chicago: Chicago University Press

Norwegian Black Metallers as there is no mention of propensity to commit transgressive behaviour; which while useful in that it helps us to envision the Norwegian groups as centred around the sonic output instead of the minority who committed the criminal offences, also contains the disadvantage of not helping to explain the reasoning behind the transgressions in terms of gang activity.

Klein later, however, redefined gangs to three more concise points; they must be recognised by those outside the groups, such as neighbourhood residents; they must recognisable themselves normally with a group name; and finally, to have been involved in enough anti-social or criminal behaviour to warrant negative responses from the dominant culture or authorities.[68] Although less detailed than Thrasher; it starts to divert the idea of a gang into that of a criminal gang. It has been commented that the first two criteria are easily achievable by many organised groups, including those with paid memberships[69] (which is the antithesis to the idea of a gang). The third criterion is what makes a criminal, or at the very least an anti-social, gang. This definition is fairly useless in this context, as it is too wide-ranging and therefore highly fallible. Later, it was suggested in Ball & Curry that the realm of gang research should fall within the area of phenomenology, and the important areas to be uncovered were those that were unique to the subjects in question as opposed to the "normative content."[70] Effectively, over-turning Klein and Thrasher, when it came to light that there had been so many attempts to define the term 'gang' and met with so little success, but maintaining their regard to the symbols, behavioural patterns and cultural caveats, that make so many of the gangs unique is precisely what can be used to prove a connection.[71] Consequently, the symbols that make the Norwegian Black Metal Scene a gang, must be unique and differentiated from others, but must be similar enough to be relied upon for reflexivity.

When considering the Norwegian Black Metal Scene as a gang, I will use Thrasher's classic definition, as it emanates the most conclusively in its nature, and later, Klein's definition, as it suggests us some disparaging inconsistencies. If once again, we are to refer to Thrasher's defining points; he expresses that a gang must have an "unplanned origin." Depending on the definition of "unplanned," this can be used to apply to the Black Metal Scene, as when Aarseth formed 'Mayhem,' he could not have had any idea that people would share the enthusiasm for his product to the extent that they did (Kristiansen: 2010). The earliest demos with 'Dead' on vocals were distributed in the same manner as many tapes, through the 'Slayer' fanzine,[72] without the blatant fanaticism that the reviewer Jon Kristiansen ('Metalion' Editor of 'Slayer' fanzine) exhibited in the article,[73] Mayhem's new strain of aural terrorism would never have reached an audience, and never have been memically reproduced[74] ('Darkthrone's' first demo album: "Goatlord," and first album proper: "Soulside Journey," was heavily inspired by the Stockholm Death Metal bands: 'Carnage' and 'Nihilist').[75] Secondly, there was

---

[68] Klein, M. W., (1971), Street Gangs and Street Workers, New Jersey: Prentice Hall

[69] Bursik, R. J., Gramsick, H. G., (1993), *Neighbourhoods and Crime: The dimensions of effective community control*, New York: Lexington Books

[70] Ball, R. A., Curry, G. D., (1995), "The logic of definition in criminology: Purposes and methods for defining gangs," *Criminology*, 33, 225-245

[71] Curry, G. D., Decker, S. H., (1998), *Confronting Gangs: Crime and community*, Los Angeles: Roxbury

[72] 'Fanzine,' refers to an amateur magazine, often cut and pasted articles over Xeroxed photographs that covered underground bands at that time. Until the explosion of the internet, the fanzines were the only way to find out about underground bands, see: Wagner, J., (2010), *Mean Deviation: Four Decades of Progressive Heavy Metal*, Brooklyn: Bazillion Points.

[73] Kristiansen, J., (1992), "Mayhem," *Slayer Issues 3&4: A Thrash Metal Attack,* Sarpsborg: Self-published

[74] Hoare, J., (2009), "Left Hand Pathfinders". *Terrorizer* #182, London: Dark Arts Ltd.

clear face to face interaction, as the groups would play with each other, and trades tapes. There was a morale which resulted in elevating the group above a mob; this was simply that of the "evil and darkness," although there was variation here, in that some proponents such as Vikernes were more indoctrinated than others like Fenriz. So it cannot truly be said that this solidarity was shared among all members. The "common tradition" in this gang would effectively be the Black Metal music that each played; although each band played their interpretation of it, the sonic template would combine the bands. As already mentioned the location preferred by the groups became Oslo itself, as bands outside of Oslo however active, were never considered in the same light. So far, it is apparent that the Black Metal troops almost closely constitute a gang. Unfortunately, however, if we consider for a moment the recognition aspects of Klein's proposition; unless the groups were at shows and in full corpse paint, it is unlikely that outsiders would be able to differentiate a 'Mayhem' fan from a 'Metallica' fan (both are stereotyped by long hair and black clothes) and the groups themselves only real tenable link was the Black Metal music, nothing more.

Neo-Tribal Theory

Authors such as Spracklen[76] have identified that music scenes correspond to Maffesoli's "Neo-Tribe" label.[77] Neo-tribalism can be described as the personal rejection of mass society in favour of smaller social networks that people can connect to at a more personal level, held together by common passions or emotion and while this tenuous inter-personal link is unstable[78] at best, it remains more central to a person's being than membership of a mass society, although remaining concurrent with mass society is also a feature.[79] Putnam suggests that an individual's connection to mass society will decline due to the ever-increasing distance one has from it. In an age when one will happily commute an hour for work, living in ever greater distances from the opportunity for social interaction, and frequent movement in pursuit of economic benefit, and the lack of emphasis on social conduct and bonds of friendship, are all contributing factors towards the slow weakening of connections to mass society life.[80] A prominent feature of neo-tribalism is shared consumption habits of ideologies and possessions,[81] similar to subcultures. Unlike subcultures and gangs who ostensibly maintain their presence amongst the mass culture, members of a neo-tribe are submerged in everyday life, and only occur as a visual phenomenon rarely,[82] i.e., when going to concerts.[83] Essentially neo-tribes are the results of post-modernity affecting consumption and identity formation habits.[84]

---

[75] Ekeroth, D., (2008), *Swedish Death Metal*, Brooklyn: Bazillion Points

[76] Spracklen, K., (2010), "True Aryan Black Metal: The Meaning of Leisure, Belonging and Construction of Whiteness in Black Metal Music," *The Metal Void: First Gatherings*, Inter-Disciplinary Press

[77] Maffesoli, M., (1996), *The Time of the Tribes: The Decline of Individualism in Mass Society*, London: Sage

[78] Cova, B., (1997), "Community & Consumption: towards a definition of the 'linking value' of products or services," *European Journal of Marketing*, 31, 297-316.

[79] Bennett, A., (1999), "Subcultures or neo-tribes? Rethinking the relationship between youth, style and musical taste," *Sociology* Vol. 33 No. 3 August 1999: 599–617

[80] Putnam, R. D., (2008), E Pluribus Unum: Diversity and Community in the 21st Century," *Scandinavian Political Studies*, 30, 2, 137-174

[81] Cova, b., Cova, V., (2001), "Tribal Marketing: The tribalisation of society and its impact on the conduct of marketing," *European Journal of Marketing: Societal Marketing in 2002 & Beyond, Special Issue,* [online] Available at: http://visionarymarketing.com/_repository/wanadoo/cova-tribe-2001.pdf

[82] Mirosa, M., (2005), "Neo-Tribal Consumption of Ideologies: Insights from new social movement theory," University of Otago, [online] Available at: http://otago.academia.edu/MirandaMirosa/Papers/367078/Neo-Tribal_Consumption_of_Ideologies_Insights_From_New_Social_Movement_Theory

In the case of most Music-based youth subcultures (Mods, Rockers, etc.), the base material (social context, class structure, garments etc) could be split from the music and engineered into its own distinct entity; that of an aesthetically discernible fashion. Thus by the commercialisation of the subculture, it expands, but consequently dilutes, as the style drifts further away from its principal meaning.[85] The same cannot be said of the Black Metal subculture as the components of the culture are intertwined to the point that separation immediately severs the meaning. We must remember that the Norwegian Black Metal scene was a construction of what the Scene Leaders heard and felt, be it first wave Black Metal such as Celtic Frost and Bathory or the general dissatisfaction and anger at the Christianity that emitted unethical amounts of power over them (Moynihan, Soderlind: 2003). The dissections of such elements become separate entities in their own right, and are unrecognisable as Norwegian Black Metal. Hence, allegiance to the Black Metal subculture takes a higher level of conscious choice than neo-tribal cultures require. Although considering the idea of being generally invisible to mainstream society, except for in certain cases, the Norwegian Black Metal Scene rings true to this component. It wasn't until the crimes began to happen that the outside world began to pay attention to the Black Metal Underground, and stopped dismissing them as another group of disenfranchised music-obsessed teenagers (Baddeley: 2010). Another failure of the neo-tribal label when applied to Black Metal is that of the lack of social interaction, assuming that the group communicated face-to-face rarely, and lived in geographically diverse areas. The social ties that held the Metallers together were far stronger, and meeting points in Oslo such as Helvete, were popular hangouts for exchange of knowledge of underground bands etc. (Kristiansen: 2011).

Chapter II Conclusion

Throughout this chapter we have observed how the Norwegian Black Metal Underground Scene functioned and flourished throughout the 1990's. I have described the divergence between two of the Scene's leaders (after the death of Euronymous) as Vikernes chose to induct political machinations into his 'Burzum' project and Fenriz chose to forego politics and carry on purely concentrating on his music and championing underground bands, so we therefore have seen that allegiance to Black Metal meant many different things to different individuals. With this information, it is easier to conclude that there is no single subcultural model that fits the Norwegian Scene, as the closest approximation is Thrasher's gang model, but even this fails when the variation in behaviour exhibited by scene members comes to the forefront. The Satanic Metal Underground was therefore entirely unique in its existence. It can be said that the nature of the transgressions (social and criminal) was promoted by members of the scene seeking to perform acts that would constantly increase in their extremity, thus memically reproducing and re-enforcing the more extreme ideas of the subculture. Inside the group, they clearly believed that they could and should transcend boundaries in their acts of rebellion. However, it must be re-enforced that with any subculture/gang/neo-tribe, the most important feature is that of each participant's belonging. Without the conscious act of belonging as opposed to the mass society rejection, a subculture

---

[83] Perdue, D., Durrschmidt, J., Jowers, P., Doherty, R., (1997), "DIY culture and extended milieux: LETS, veggie boxes and festivals," *The Sociological Review,* 431-441

[84] Patterson, M., (1998) "Direct marketing in postmodernity: neo-tribes and direct communications", *Marketing Intelligence & Planning,* Vol. 16, 1, pp.68 - 74

[85] Savage, J., (1992), *England's Dreaming: Anarchy, Sex Pistols, Punk Rock and Beyond,* London: St. Martin's Press

cannot take hold.[86] This paper does not intend to focus individually on the acts themselves nor the perpetrators, or even the musical output, but combine the tenets and visualize in the reader's mind, that all three components are an important factor in understanding just how the scene became active and where the politicisation came from.

---

[86] Overell, R., (2010), "Brutal belonging in Melbourne's Grindcore Scene," *Studies in Symbolic Interaction,* 35, 79-99

Trve: The Norwegian Black Metal Scene: A Subcultural study of Transgression through Music.

Fig. 3, Per Yngve Ohlin "Dead" in the basement of Helvete, circa 1991

Chapter III: The Transgressions Committed inside the Scene and the Explosion on to the World Stage.

This chapter will take each transgressive act and analyse the events that occurred in the aftermath, along with excerpts from interviews with members of the scene who held significant social capital. In this way we can develop a visualisation of to what degree the subculture functioned on acts of extremity and how notoriety grew. I will also address the issues of the culture's ideas of theistic Satanism as it is an important concept to grasp when evaluating the burnings of the multiple churches across Scandinavia.

There are numerous arguments that such an abrasive, confrontational form of music as Black Metal would never have gained the success and exposure that it did without the exploits of those constructing it from a small clan in Norway. As previously mentioned, Necro Butcher believes that it was Ohlin's suicide that commenced outside interest in primarily the subculture, the expansion of the consumption of their music, being a by-product. The roots of the scene began as far back as the formation of Mayhem in 1984, as a band simply regurgitating what they had heard from Venom. It was at this stage in Mayhem's formation that the newfound strain of Satanism, which they mistakenly believed to be central to Venom's message, had taken root among the Norwegian youth movement.

Satanism in the Norwegian Black Metal Scene versus Recognised Legitimate Satanism

Satanism amongst the Norwegian Black Metal subculture was a fluid concept, not existing as a solidly conscious worship of a theistic "Satan," but more accurately defined as a direct rejection of their Christian upbringing in the most objectionable and reprehensible method possible and returning humanity to their original bestial nature.[87] Due to their age, the knowledge of Satanism

---

[87]

was limited to what they had accrued through Christian teachings. Hence their interpretation of Satanism simply involved rejection of anything perceived as morally "good" and sanctioned in the bible. For example, notable Black Metal band 'Gorgoroth' named their 2006 album: 'Ad Majorem Sathanas Gloriam'[88] meaning 'for the greater glory of Satan'[89] which itself is a subversion of the monastic group, the "Society of Jesus'" motto 'Ad Majorem Dei Gloriam.'[90] Upon being questioned in Until the Light Takes Us, about Aarseth's belief, Vikernes commented:

> *"Ostensibly, the theistic Satanism embraced by Euronymous was a deliberate fundamental inversion of Roman Catholic dogma, fully supporting what was found to be abhorrent and blasphemous: for instance, he was an ardent proponent of sodomy, rape and murder simply because they were evil acts. He opposed the teachings of Aleister Crowley and Anton LaVey, for unlike Euronymous they promoted what he saw as 'peace', and commercial frivolity, as well as individualism in contrast to precedence of dogma (although Crowley and LaVey both included dogma in their belief systems, they were also naturally opposed to the subservience that Euronymous promoted)."* [91]

I have already explained the limits that subculture members such as Euronymous would go to, to perform blasphemous acts. The nature of these extreme acts that were performed in the name of Satanism, were by their very character shocking, and wilfully disobedient in the face of the political power that Christianity holds in Norway. The acts themselves can be considered more acts of defiance than satanic rituals; the blasphemies were private in nature and in no way intended to shock outsiders or gain notoriety at this stage. In fact there was never any attempt made by the subculture leaders to convert outsiders. They wholly believed in the exclusivity of what they had created, going as far as to treat casual shoppers at Helvete with disdain (Aites, Ewell: 2009. Due to the random variety of the blasphemous transgressions they enacted, it is unlikely that they were corresponding to recognisable demonic worship. The groups themselves preferred to identify their acts as "acts of war" against the powers of Norway.

Satanism in its most legitimate form; practiced by such establishments as the Church of Satan and The Temple of Set all profuse to follow the "Left Hand Path."[92] The term "Left Hand Path" symbolises the "opposite" philosophy in the dichotomous spectrum of Western Hermeticism, or the Western Esoteric Tradition.[93] The "Right Hand Path" indicates denominations of Judaeo-Christianity amongst other minor religious sects.[94] The group rejects the Christian ideas of mercy and abstinence, and concentrates on fulfilling the desires of the self. Even with these idiosyncrasies in place, the satanic rites can be seen as ethical,[95] (See Appendix II for satanic rites) representing similar moral

---

[88] Gorgoroth, (2006), *Ad Majorem Sathanas Gloriam*, Regain Records

[89] Shakespeare, S., (2010), "The Light That Illuminates Itself, the dark that soils itself: Blackened notes from Schelling's Underground," *Hideous Gnosis: Black Metal Theory Symposium I*, New York: Createspace

[90] Wright, J., (2005), *God's Soldiers: Adventure, Politics, Intrigue and Power- A History of the Jesuits*, New York: Image

[91] Aites, A., Ewell, A., (2009), "Interview with Varg Vikernes from Trondheim Prison," *Until the Light Takes Us,*

[92] Flowers, S., (1997), *Lords of the Left Hand Path: A History of Spiritual Dissent*. Runa Raven Press.

[93] Evans, D., (2007), *The History of British Magick After Crowley*, Hidden Publishing.

[94] Kupperman, J. S., (2001) "A History of the Western Mystery Tradition to the Twentieth Century: The Mythology of Magic," *Journal of The Western Mystery Tradition*, Vol. 0, [online] Available at: http://www.jwmt.org/v1n0/history.html

[95] Aquino, M., (2009), *Church of Satan: Sixth Edition*, [online] Available at: http://www.xeper.org/maquino/nm/COS.pdf

values to those of Christianity. However, when considering the inclusion and expectations of self-indulgence inherent in Satanism, ironically it can be argued that Satanism represents far less punitiveness than Judaeo-Christian denominations.

Although the obvious link between each strain of Satanism is a shared a belief in a satanic force, be it theistic or esoteric, they also both exemplified the exclusivity that the religion offered. Anton LaVey commented: "Satanists are born, they are not made," indicating that Satanism unlike the teachings of other religions was never meant for the masses, and is not defined as an all-encompassing answer. This leaves LaVey's Satanists with an acute sense of respect for those that follow other belief structures. The youth Satanists in Mayhem et al. weren't at all concerned with converting outsiders, preferring to maintain their "Satanic Metal Underground." This is clearly where the divergence lies between the respectful "Laveyan" tenets and the nihilistic, anarchic beliefs that the Black Metal movement adopted, which composed of little more than what Euronymous saw as TRVE.

The Norwegian Satanic Church Burnings

This brand of satanic worship has been linked to the arson attacks on 50 Christian churches in Norway between 1992 and 1996, all committed by the pseudo-satanic youth members of the Black Metal subculture, and later, their fans.[96] This is clearly the most visual representation of transgression due to the sheer volume of Christian churches that were raised to the ground in arson attacks. The aforementioned attacks have been divisive among the Black Metal community, with equal proponents and detractors. The surviving members of the subculture are divided on the true motives of these attacks: The most visual representation of transgression arrived in the sheer volume of Christian churches that were raised to the ground in arson attacks. Between the years 1992 and 1996 50 churches in Norway were destroyed by deliberate attacks by the pseudo-satanic youth (Torstein: 1998). The surviving members of the subculture are divided on the true motives of these attacks: Gaahl and Roger Tiegs (aka 'Infernus' guitarist of 'Gorgoroth') celebrate the burnings and have been noted as exclaiming: *"There should have been more of them, and there will be more of them."*[97] Equally however, Jorn Stubberud (aka 'Necro butcher' current bass player with 'Mayhem') and Kjetil Manheim (aka 'Manheim' ex-drummer of Mayhem) have removed themselves from the argument stating that: *"It was just people trying to gain acceptance within a strict group ... they wanted some sort of approval and status."* Thus, disapproving of the burnings and ridiculing the reasons behind them.[98]

However, blaming the fans for re-interpreting the actions of the groups themselves cannot really be blamed on the musicians.[99] Both sides agree, however, that far from being directly linked to dissent from the patriarchal Christian society, the arson attacks were the result of a combination of reasons that some perpetrators responded to more than others.

---

[96] Torstein, G., (1998), *Satan Rides The Media.*

[97] Dunn, S., (2005) *Metal: A Headbanger's Journey,* clip available online at:
http://www.youtube.com/watch?v=oQJqZFUell8

[98] Aasdal, P., Ledang, M., (2008), *Once Upon a Time in Norway.*

[99] Sampar, M., (2005), "Rock n Roll Suicide: Why Heavy Metal musicians cannot be blamed for the violent acts of their listeners," Seton Hall Journal of Sports and Entertainment Law, 15, 173-196.

The churches themselves, many dating back to the 12th Century (when Christianity and Lutheran Catholicism had taken hold in Scandinavia) were Stave Churches.[100] These imposing buildings were far from faceless, archaic symbols of Christianity, but were beautiful, individual constructions[101] that were a beacon for Nordic travellers and culturally aware tourists. The most famous casualty was *Fantoft Stave* Church, Bergen, one of the first to be attacked by arsonists representing the Black Metal subculture on 6th June 1992. Varg Vikernes has been suspected of the attack since the crime itself,[102] but there has never been sufficient proof, although he was charged and imprisoned for the burnings of three others, running concurrently with the murder charge for killing Aarseth. The burnt ruins of *Fantoft Stavkirke* appear on the cover of Burzum's second release: "Aske"[103] (meaning: Ashes) and many believe that Vikernes took the photograph himself after committing the crime. A deeply suspicious act, especially since the first 1,000 copies of "Aske" were distributed alongside a cigarette lighter bearing the same photograph of the charred remains. He has even offered a "theory" on the attack, claiming it was "retaliation to a Christian church built on sacred Pagan grounds." [104]

The Norse race's origins in paganism were transformed from historic tales of heroism into mythology. Classic Norwegian folk songs were given new Christian lyrics, and Christian morals. The ancient stories were twisted to fit the parameters of the new religion, and the Pagan holidays had been replaced. Paganism had been subtly usurped by Christianity.[105] Although it has not been completely forgotten and survives in myth and folklore, it is believed that because of the sheer insistence of integrity of those old storytellers, true Norse mythologies remain almost identical to their original forms. This is comparable to the Greek mythologies; whose Gods in classic translation were malevolent and cruel, and over time were evolved to satisfy the needs of new audiences, becoming harmless and benevolent. Norwegian Gods have always been violent and bloodthirsty and are still recognised today as such.[106] These stories evoke immense pride in those of Nordic descent,[107] but after Christianity arrived in Scandinavia; the Pagan Gods were displaced and with them, the identities of the Norse men and women dissipated too. Vikernes is a passionate believer that the "Judaeo-Christian" religion had no respect for the pagans, and therefore why should the pagans have any respect for theirs? (Aites Ewell: 2009). This lack of respect was part of the root cause for the arson attacks, and how they were carried out with such ease and disdain for the buildings they were destroying. Although Vikernes acknowledges the beauty of the architecture, the symbolic value was, for him, far too disgusting to excuse. Vikernes also stated that due to the vast power that Christianity held over Norway, the church was not just a symbol of religious power, but a

---

[100] Medieval, all-wooden designs; consisting of a post and beam construction or "stav" in Norwegian. Once commonplace all over North-western Europe, now principally associated with Norway.

[101] Hohler, E. B., (1999). *Norwegian Stave Church Sculpture*. Oslo: Scandinavian University Press

[102] Christie, I., (2003). *Sound of the Beast: the Complete Headbanging History of Heavy Metal*. New York: HarperCollins Publishers Inc.

[103] Aske, (1993), Deathlike Silence Productions.

[104] Campion, C., (2005), "In the Face of Death," *The Observer,* [online] Available at: http://www.guardian.co.uk/music/2005/feb/20/popandrock4

[105] Kristiansen, J., (2008), "An Introduction to True Norwegian Black Metal" *True Norwegian Black Metal,* London: Vice

[106] Dasent, Sir G. W., (1859), *Popular Tales From The Norse, (Norske Folkeeventyr)* [online] Available at: http://www.gutenberg.org/catalog/world/readfile?fk_files=1472615

[107] Abram, C., (2011). *Myths of the Pagan North: the Gods of the Norsemen*, London: Continuum

representative of Government and, therefore the ultimate symbol of Societal Control. Hence, upon considering the arson attacks, he believed he was effectively attacking both institutions.[108]

Euronymous viewed himself as the Norwegian Black Metaller's "godfather" and saw it as necessary that he remained merely in an organisational role, and if he got involved in the church burnings, the ramifications would be profoundly negative on the Scene as a whole.[109] Euronymous took a different view of the arson attacks; he viewed them as generating societal dividing lines, helping to further his ideal "Us-versus-them" campaign, which was principle to the Black Metal movement. This observation was ratified by the Priest Rolf Armand Rasmussen, whose parish church, 'Asane,' was raised to the ground in 1992. He reported an increase in the congregation and a new union of the people (Beste: 2008).

Vikernes now claims the media jumped on the satanic aspect of the subculture and that he never truly believed in a satanic deity (but he is notorious for altering claims in interviews) (Baddeley: 2010). It is believed that after the initial burnings which were simple arson attacks committed by amongst others; Vikernes 'Faust' eventually, the attacks became an act by the fans to attain "notoriety within the scene"- according to Manheim and Stubberud. This change can be attributed partially to the media's insistence on painting all activities within the scene as being committed by violent Satanists. This status correlated fittingly with the bored youth of Norway, and they were only too happy to adopt it. At this point, the ideas central to the defiant character of the arson were shifted; the attacks became as Vikernes notes, the acts of "a bunch of brain-dead metal heads"[110] (Aites, Ewell: 2009). It has been attested that the violent actions of Heavy Metal fans cannot be attributed to the bands themselves, (Sampar: 2005) due to the tenuous link between the two parties. The further away geographically the Churches stand from Oslo, the centre of the subculture, reinforces this distinction. The fact that the attacks were picked up and re-interpreted; gives strength to the truism that the youth inside the scene weren't the only ones at the time who were disillusioned with the "ultra-liberal but ultra-conformist" state of affairs in Norway (Aites, Ewell: 2009). It is also worth noting that arson on stave churches is an incredibly easy task to perform due to their completely wooden construction (Hohler: 1999) and they leave an incredibly dramatic image as they immolate (Aites, Ewell: 2009). Therefore, it can be seen as an extremely effective outcome with a minimum of effort involved, hence a perfect motif for youthful defiance.

The Suicide of "Dead," The Murder of Aarseth by Vikernes and Faust's killing

Prior to the arson attacks, the scene had already proved controversial at an international level with the suicide of emigrated Swedish vocalist Per Yngve Ohlin on 8th April 1991 (aka 'Dead' ex-vocalist of 'Mayhem'). Ohlin shot himself in the head with a shotgun and bullets given to him by Varg Vikernes and left a suicide note apologizing for the mess. The first to arrive at the site was Aarseth whose first response was to take photographs of the scene and to steal remnants of Ohlin's shattered skull to make necklaces; that he gave to Black Metal Scene members that he deemed "worthy" (Aites, Ewell: 2009). Rumours also reported that he made soup from segments of Ohlin's brain, although they turned out to be false. This is infamously the first "event" that created the subculture's notoriety. In interviews regarding Ohlin's suicide it has been credited as such: Necro Butcher (offered that:

---

[108] Beste, P., (2008), *True Norwegian Black Metal*, London: Vice
[109] Arnopp, J., (1993), "We are but slaves of the one with horns," *Kerrang! Magazine*, No. 463, 27/03/1993
[110] A term used to describe metal devotees.

"people became more aware of the [black metal] scene after Dead had shot himself … I think it was Dead's suicide that really changed the scene".[111]

If this was the trigger that brought Black Metal to the World's attention, then the subsequent events served greater purpose. Ohlin was a young Swedish man, who before emigrating to Norway for the sole purpose of replacing Sven Erik Kristiansen (aka 'Maniac,' ex-vocalist of 'Mayhem') in the band, sang in a Swedish death metal called 'Morbid.' He was described by Bard G. Eithun as:

> *"He [Dead] wasn't a guy you could know very well. I think even the other guys in Mayhem didn't know him very well. He was hard to get close to. I met him two weeks before he died. I'd met him maybe six to eight times, in all. He had lots of weird ideas. I remember Aarseth was talking about him and said he did not have any humour. He did, but it was very obscure.[112] Honestly, I don't think he was enjoying living in this world, which of course resulted in the suicide."[113]*

By all accounts, Ohlin had more than his fair share of idiosyncrasies: famously burying his stage clothes and digging them up prior to playing concerts, so that they would have the "grave scent;"[114] starving himself just to appear sick and wounded and notoriously carried around a dead crow in a bag which he would smell before a show, so he could perform with the smell of "death in his nostrils" (Campion: 2005). He was known among the subculture for this line taken from his suicide note: "I am not a human. This is just a dream and soon I will awake. It was too cold and my blood was frozen all the time."[115] It was believed that Ohlin had experienced a near death experience in his childhood, and wished to return to that state (Kristiansen: 2008). Ohlin did not believe himself to be human, but a force of nature from another world (Moynihan, Soderlind: 2003). Hence it can be argued that his suicide should not be considered as an extreme act, aside from the reaction that resonated through the subculture and the subsequent bleeding effect into the mainstream consciousness.

Aarseth reported that Ohlin had been a casualty of the transition between old and new extreme music scenes;[116] voicing his disgust at how bands like "Morbid Angel[117] now appeared on MTV" through the suicide of Ohlin. Euronymous like many others made allusions to the good old days, before the "music business got involved." He maintains that Ohlin existed for the "TRVE Black Metal lifestyle" and refused to live among this new scene, although throughout Ohlin's life there was never any evidence of this holding true. It was another of the many examples throughout Euronymous' life where he would manipulate events for his own benefit. Desperate to be seen as the member of the Black Metal subculture with the most accumulated social capital, to the point where Vikernes

---

[111] "Unrestrained" Magazine, #15, "Interview with Necrobutcher" www.unrestrainedmag.com (Defunct) NB. Many interviews with Black Metal scene members were featured in "fanzines" which have long been rendered defunct.

[112] For example Dead's suicide note apologises for the mess.

[113] Moynihan, M., Soderlind, D., (2003), *Lords of Chaos*, 2nd Edition, Feral House,

[114] Hellhammer interviewed by Dmitry Basik (June 1998)

[115] www.peryngveohlin.com/frames3.htm

[116] Sanchez, R. C., (1992), "Dead & Buried: Mayhem" *Terrorizer Magazine: Black Metal Special #128,* Dark Arts Ltd: London.

[117] Seminal Floridian Death Metal band, Black and Death Metal scenes clashed frequently over the latter's lack of "evil."

became aware of his manipulative nature through Aarseth's appearing to organize the church burnings, but never actually taking part. (Aites, Ewell: 2009).

On 21st August 1992, Bard G. Eithun brutally stabbed a homosexual man identified as Magne Andreassen, in Lillehammer, Norway. Eithun declared there was no real reason behind the murder, and that the music which he was famed for had not contributed to his crime (Moynihan, Soderlind: 2003). He had become physically agitated after being approached by Andreassen who was looking for sex; the combination of agitation and "morbid curiosity" about how it would feel to commit a murder led to the fatal stabbing. Andreassen is remembered as the sole, direct human victim of the Norwegian Black Metal subculture who wasn't an active participant. Andreassen enjoyed regularly walking through an area of parkland and accosting other men for sex. On that night; Andreassen met Eithun in the woods and asked him to "go for a walk." Eithun agreed, and the two disappeared into the woods, only for Magneassen's body to be found a day later with 37 stab wounds and a massive head injury as a result of repetitive kicking (Torstein: 1998). Eithun was sentenced to 14 years in prison, but served just over 9 and was released in 2003.

The media picked up on the crime as another satanic murder, but Eithun argues that he experienced "Homosexual Panic" and was driven to the point by shock and distress. Whether as a society we accept "homosexual panic defence[118]" as anything more than an archaic piece of thinly-veiled reinforcement of masculinity at legal level.[119] The jury clearly did, refusing to mete out the full extent of the sentence available, which in Norway is 21 years, to a member of that reviled band of folk devils[120]- The Norwegian Black Metallers.

In response to the satanic murder connotations, Eithun claims he never identified himself as a fascist or a Satanist and the crime was unconnected to Satanism, fascism or black metal. He claims that while in prison he put the hate and negativity out of his mind as: "Those feelings just eat you up from inside."[121] Friends such as Manheim have commented on how difficult the situation Eithun was in that led to his murder (Aasdal, Ledang: 2008). However, Jan Axel Bloomberg (aka 'Hellhammer' drummer with 'Mayhem'), a scene member notorious for making racist and homophobic comments praised Eithun for "killing that f****** faggot" (Aites, Ewell: 2009). Indicating that homophobic beliefs that may not have existed within Eithun, but were certainly active within Hellhammer. When such a prominent member makes recorded statements such as these, it is easily generalised to a whole scene.

The third notorious act which the scene will be most remembered for was the murder committed on August 10th 1993, when Vikernes stabbed Aarseth to death outside Aarseth's apartment. It is still a mystery as to the motives were for the killing, but it has recently come to light that Aarseth may

---

[118] Suffredini, K. S., (2001), "Pride & Prejudice: The Homosexual Panic Defence" *Third World L. J.*, 21, 279, [online] Available at:
http://heinonline.org/HOL/LandingPage?collection=journals&handle=hein.journals/bctw21&div=13&id=&page=

[119] Comstock, G. D., (1992), "Dismantling The Homosexual Panic Defence," *Law & Sexuality Rev. Lesbian and Gay Legal Issues,* 81, 2, [online] Available at:
http://heinonline.org/HOL/LandingPage?collection=journals&handle=hein.journals/lsex2&div=10&id=&page=
[120] Cohen, S., (2002), *Folk Devils & Moral Panics*, 3rd Edition Routledge: New York.
[121] Bowar, C., (2005), *Interview with Bard G. Eithun*, [online] Available at:
http://heavymetal.about.com/od/interviews/a/faust.htm

have been planning to "get rid" of Vikernes. If true it would give Vikernes' argument of self-defence certain justification. Aarseth's body was found in his apartment block with two stab marks in the head, five to the neck and sixteen on his back. From Vikernes' version of events; he had driven along with Snorre Ruch (ex-guitarist with 'Mayhem' also of 'Thorns') from Bergen, to Aarseth's apartment in Oslo, to sign contracts relating to Vikernes' 'Burzum's' commitment to Aarseth's record label Deathlike Silence (through which many of the early Norwegian Black Metal records were released). Rumours had been circulating that Aarseth was planning to "get rid of" Vikernes, so he, instead of requesting the contracts to be mailed direct, decided to visit Aarseth. Upon their arrival, they were granted entry to the apartment block by Aarseth, who met them wearing nothing but his underwear. At which point Aarseth attacked Vikernes and then turned to run to his bedroom, which Vikernes claims to believe that Euronymous intended to retrieve his shotgun from (the same shotgun that Ohlin had killed himself with a year previously). It was later apparent that the shotgun was not in the apartment at all, but due to Vikernes' belief that it was, he had decided to arm himself with a small fishing knife. Aarseth ran out of his apartment and down the stairs, breaking a glass lampshade (explaining the stab marks on his back) and eventually as he turned to finally attack Vikernes, he was stabbed in the skull.[122]

Vikernes received the full twenty-one year sentence that is applicable in Norwegian law for the murder and the burning of three churches. Although he surmounts to be due to the courts making an example of him: "not to mess with the mother-pig" (Vikernes: 2005), which in truth is contestable, as the previous murder by Bard G. Eithun, who was also a convicted church arsonist, a prominent scene member and had committed a gruesome hate-crime unprovoked, only received fourteen years. Ruch received 8 years for his part in "being an accomplice." According to Vikernes, his condemnation was due to Ruch being "in the wrong place at the wrong time" (Vikernes contests that there was no plan to kill Aarseth when Ruch agreed to accompany Varg). In hindsight, it is still shocking that upon hearing Varg describe the murder in the amount of detail he does, that he can be so dismissive and factual of the murder, while still maintaining elements of respect for what Euronymous accomplished for the subculture. He was very aware of Euronymous' devious nature in maintaining an image of a violent, extreme figure that lay so far away from the truth (Aites, Ewell: 2009).

News of this satanic killing reverberated around the world, culminating in a media storm, and a famous 6-page spread in UK weekly rock/metal magazine "Kerrang!" (March 1993). The article, as to be expected, contained a collection of edited quotes and sensationalist journalism depicting the Black Metal Scene as a vicious subculture of satanic worship, death and depravity. One would have expected at least a little sympathy for a magazine that specialises in "rock/metal," but to no avail. Even luminaries such as Digby Pearson, owner of Earache Records,[123] located in Nottingham, England, who has been paramount in the growth of Grindcore[124] and Death Metal[125] bands such as

---

[122] Vikernes, V., (2004), "Part II: Euronymous," *A Burzum Story*, www.burzum.org
[123] Earache Records is a record label that specialises in extreme metal, and is notable for releasing many of the early, classic records of the genre.
[124] A progression of hardcore punk, beginning in the late 1980s, consists of heavily de-tuned, distorted guitars, blast beats and screamed or growled vocals, and extreme tempos and other chaotic elements, completely dismissive of song structure. The term was coined by Napalm Death's Shane Embury.
[125] A progression of thrash metal, beginning in the mid- 1980's, once again consists of: heavily de-tuned, distorted guitars, blast beats and screamed or growled vocals, but far more focus on structure. The term is

Napalm Death, Carcass, Extreme Noise Terror, Morbid Angel and Entombed,[126] was reticent about signing Black Metal bands to his label, due to the negative press that surrounded the Norwegian strain of Black Metal that had recently spread to the genre as a whole.[127] The same man is also responsible for the worldwide release of early albums by satanic bands Deicide and Akercocke. It is clear that the anti-Christian slant was of little consequence to Earache Records and that there were real concerns about the political undercurrent inherent in the outsider's view of the scene.

Eventually, countless scene members began to show traces of far-right political beliefs, some even going as far as describing themselves as followers of Nazism. The most notable antagonist being Varg Vikernes himself, whose racist rants are well publicized in document form and online archives.[128] When one considers these heinous activities plus the burnings of countless churches across Norway and into Sweden, which various members have attested to participating in, the media have implied that the music contributed to the atrocities, since the only common factors between all events is the Black Metal music that all consumed and played, and the scene they were a part of.

Chapter III Conclusion

Gaahl has stated in interview that:

> *'Black Metal was never meant to reach an audience. It was purely for our own satisfaction, something entirely self-centred. The shared goal was to become the true Satan; the elite human, basically. The elite are above rules. So people did what they wanted to do. And they had a common enemy which was, of course, Christianity, socialism and everything that democracy stands for, especially this idea that every man is alike and equal to his neighbour. That, of course, is a fake.* (Campion: 2005)

This description of the Black Metal Satanism is useful in understanding just where the negativity towards outsiders arrives from. Politically, this places the subculture to the extreme right, and also offers a theory into why transgressions were so freely committed. In trying to become "elite humans," the laws of society were not only broken, but had lost all meaning. The justification for the transgressions was simply that the laws of non-elite humans no longer applied. However, it was always obvious that the offenders would eventually receive their punishments at the hands of the justice system they had denied to adhere to. Problematically, it is a worrying concept that at this point in Norway the laws functioned only to punish the Black Metal-affiliated offenders. In no way did the laws prevent the atrocities from happening. It can be argued that by denying the law by stating a transcendental stance, one becomes completely lawless. Justice merely serves to attempt to catch-up and mete out retribution. Gaahl's comments regarding Black Metal not intending to reach an audience and as something entirely self-centred echoes LaVey's words about Satanism as not being a religion for the majority, and its self-serving nature. So in effect, the two breeds of Satanism that diverges at almost every point both have self-satisfaction as a central idea.

---

believed to have originated as the title of US band Possessed's 1984 demo.

[126] Scwarz, P., (2000), *Foreseeing the Future of Music*, [online] Available at:
http://www.chroniclesofchaos.com/articles/chats/1-291_earache_records.aspx

[127] Mudrian, A., (2004), *Choosing Death: The Improbable History of Death Metal and Grindcore*, Washington: Feral House.

[128] Please see: http://www.burzum.org/eng/library/

If we can consider for one moment that the Black Metal subculture as not a pathology from normality, but a normality in itself, it is only the minority that chose to supplant the status quo and behave ever more extremely in pursuit of their goals. The limits pushed by Vikernes, Aarseth and Eithun should not be taken as reflective of an entire subculture. Eithun still maintains that his murder wasn't driven by Satanism or Black Metal but "perhaps being surrounded by all that hatred made it easier," (Aites, Ewell: 2009). For the majority of the Black Metal Scene, any societal rules were subverted and challenged by musical output and aesthetic alone. The premiere raison d'être was the unification and the belonging afforded to a subculture.[129] Logically speaking, if a youth movement isn't offering a perceived "solution" to complexities experienced by the intended targets, it will not expand and eventually expire. The actions of the afore-mentioned scene leaders were in essence; rebelling against the rebels.

---

[129] Bettez-Halnon, K., (2006), "Heavy Metal Carnival and Dis-Alienation: The Politics of Grotesque Realism," *Symbolic Interaction*, Vol. 29, 1, pp. 33-48.

Trve: The Norwegian Black Metal Scene: A Subcultural study of Transgression through Music.

fig. 4: Bard G. "Faust" Eithun, in an early promotional shot for 'Emperor,' circa 1991

Chapter IV: The Demise of the Norwegian Black Metal Subculture and its Continuing Legacy in Music Today

In this chapter, I intend to hypothesise on the demise of the Norwegian Black Metal Scene. The end of the Scene is difficult to place on a chronological scale. However, following Euronymous' murder and the overwhelmingly negative press surrounding Vikernes' trial and sentencing and 'Mayhem's' initial disbandment in 1994, the Black Metal Scene was for the first time without its leaders, and therefore unguided. It is postulated that this is when the seeds of the Subculture's demise were sown. This is a simple theory and it is quite easily disprovable with analysis (Moynihan, Soderlind: 2003). It is unlikely that this "lack of leadership" was a major contribution to the Scene's demise, as many of the bands such as 'Emperor,' 'Enslaved,' 'Darkthrone' and 'Immortal' would (despite some line-up changes) pursue growing commercial interest, and would have been able to survive on their own impetus rather than that of Vikernes and Aarseth. To aid in my analytical discussion on the state of Norwegian Black Metal today, and just what these changes say about it, I shall also ask if anything is left of the Scene and what form it has been warped into.

The Demise of the Norwegian Black Metal Scene, or a fragmentation...

Even while imprisoned Vikernes (although for obvious reasons was denied access to stringed instruments) continued his 'Burzum' project, producing two albums, that while a serious digression from Black Metal, could only be described as "dark ambient" having been created entirely on synthesisers with a basic tape recorder (Aites, Ewell: 2009). The resulting albums: "Dauði Baldrs"[130] and "Hliðskjálf"[131] were accompanied by press releases acknowledging Vikernes' disillusionment with Black Metal[132] (echoing his earlier consternation about "brain-dead metal heads.") Upon his release, the next two albums "Belus"[133] and "Fallen"[134] (the latter being the first Burzum album with

---

[130] Dauði Baldrs, (1997),Misanthropy Records
[131] Hliðskjálf, (1999), Misanthropy Records
[132] Mitchell, C., (2005), "Interview with Varg Vikernes (10.05.2005),"*Metalcrypt E-zine,* [online] available at: http://www.burzum.org/eng/library/2005_interview_metalcrypt.shtml
[133] Belus, (2010), Byelobog Productions
[134] Fallen, (2011), Byelobog Productions

a title in English) released in 2010 and 2011, respectively show a return to the Black Metal style he had abandoned. When considering Vikernes attitude towards the media, twisting his perceptions to fit in with the story he wants to create (Baddeley: 2010), it is quite possible that those press releases were simply his unwillingness to admit that he felt crippled by the lack of access to stringed instruments. Vikernes' 'Burzum' project has reinvigorated interest in Norwegian Black Metal, however he now feels as if he "stands alone" from other Black Metal bands.[135] In this way we can begin to consider the dissolution of the Scene as a fragmentation. Today the definition of Norwegian Black Metal has expanded to include not only 'Burzum's' late 90's dark ambient opuses, but even more diverse sounds. This is further exemplified by 'Darkthrone's' 2006 album: "The Cult is Alive,"[136] in which they have infused both punk and "rock n' roll" features into their Black Metal formula. Following the reaction of critics[137] to this change, they sarcastically entitled their 2008 album: "Dark Thrones and Black Flags,"[138] referring to the seminal hardcore punk band 'Black Flag.' It is also worth nothing that 'Enslaved,' a band from Bergen, who have always experimented more progressively with their music than other Black Metal bands, now play a brand of metal which is closer to 'Bathory's' later "Viking Metal" material as well as harmonic passages reminiscent of 'Pink Floyd,' (Wagner: 2010) than their Black Metal roots. Once again, however, this sound too is now packaged alongside Norwegian Black Metal.

This fragmentation of Norwegian Black Metal has led to boundaries being re-defined. Some would argue that this alone represents the death of the subculture, but conversely the musical output which now falls under the Black Metal umbrella is more progressive, more artistically advanced and importantly, more interesting. Other results of this new Black Metal scene have been the concert line-ups that during the Scene's heyday would have been impossible. In November 2011, the band 'Gorgoroth,' will play a European tour dubbed "Under the Sign of Hell 2011," with Polish Death Metal veterans 'Vader.'[139] This pairing, due to the previous animosities between Black and Death Metal scenes would be clearly beyond the imagination of fans and bands alike, but Black Metal in the 21st Century is more inclusive, which is a clear advantage to all parties concerned, as more inclusion equates to more exposure.

If we are to assume that the Norwegian Black Metal Scene has dissolved and its remnants can no longer constitute a subculture, there is much evidence to support this argument. Youth subcultures have been a prominent feature of life since the post-war era, and the social invention of the concept of a 'teenager' (Hall, Jefferson: 2006). However, some have invariably maintained a constant existence in fringe society and others have been sudden explosions and disappear as quickly as they arrive. In the next section of this chapter, I will be comparing the Norwegian Black Metal Subculture with another youth subculture that has existed since long before the 1990's and has outlived it spectacularly, always existent on the edges of the social sphere. For the purposes of providing arguments that will exhibit that the Black Metal Subculture in Norway is long expired, I will be comparing it to the 'Goth' subculture and exposing the difference that ensure "gothic" ideas will memically reproduce where others have failed.

---

[135] Minton, J., (2010), "Interview with Varg Vikernes," Terrorizer #194, March, London: Dark Arts Ltd.
[136] The Cult Is Alive, (2006), Peaceville Records
[137] Alisoglu, S., (2006), "The Cult is Alive- Review," Blabbermouth.net, [online] available at:
http://www.roadrunnerrecords.com/blabbermouth.net/showreview.aspx?reviewID=693
[138] Dark Thrones & Black Flags, (2008), Peaceville Records.
[139] http://www.balkanconcerts.com/2011/08/gorgoroth-vader-balkan-tour-2011.html

The Norwegian Metal subculture vs. the Goth subculture

The Gothic subculture has been a mainstay in society since the early 1980's as an offshoot from the influential but short-lived post-punk scene.[140] Visually striking, the aesthetic combines 19th Century influences with modern interpretations of dark attire and fetish wear.[141] As a subculture it has shown an immense resistance to the pressures of post-modernity with little stylistic change in itself, but smaller subsidiary groups (such as "Rivetheads;" followers of the industrial music culture)[142] evolve their own style and remain static.[143] Like Black Metal, both subcultures resisted change, just like the "TRVE" Black Metallers would regard classic bands such as Venom and Bathory highly, "Batcavers,"[144] would show the same respect for stylistic icons such as; Siouxsie Soux (Savage: 1992) and Robert Smith of 'The Cure.' However, the differences between the subcultures are far more striking than similarities, and have ensured that Goths have survived for nigh-on 30 years.

A striking feature of Gothic subculture is that is succumbs to influences of art, literature, film and music. The historical influences of Edgar Allen Poe, Bram Stoker and H.P. Lovecraft have instigated the modern gothic culture, and in turn the current wave of Gothic individuals influenced the works of contemporary Gothic authors Anne Rice and Poppy Z. Brite. This interdisciplinary relationship has been a vital part in the reproduction of "Goth" throughout generations. The dialectic engagement with art and literature has provided a valuable source of vitality towards keeping the Gothic subculture alive.[145] The Black Metal Scene, conversely has seen little relationship with any outside influences aside from the Norse folktales, and the music of 'Venom,' 'Bathory' etc. The only scripture that was vaguely associated with the subculture is the Satanic Bible, which very few had a copy of (Aites, Ewell: 2009), and LaVey's Church of Satan merely laughed their advances off. This disagreement lea to a retaliation that depicted a "no fun" sign with Anton LaVey's portrait in the centre (Moynihan Soderlind: 2003). Visual artists such as Bjarne Melgaard,[146] (whose Black Metal-inspired exhibition is featured in "Until the Light Takes Us") have attempted to incorporate the cold, dark aspects into their work; along the same lines as critics faun over the "outsider art" of Henry Darger and Howard Finster, but have been met with rebuttal by the Black Metal world (In "UTLU" Fenriz's reaction to the exhibition was simply: "I f****** hate it," (Aites, Ewell: 2009)). Feeling that all he has worked towards is being re-conceptualised and made alien to him, Fenriz feels that Melgaard's work was completely against the spirit of: "we did it for ourselves." (See above). The Norwegian Black Metal Scene could not simply survive without the re-invigorating effects of outsider influence. This was not only its downfall, but also its strength; for over ten years, the Scene existed solely by itself, unaffected by the outside world, making the output as musically and idealistically pure as it could possibly be.[147]

---

[140] Baddeley, G., (2002), *Goth Chic: A Connoisseur's Guide to Dark Culture,* London: Plexus Publishing Ltd

[141] Mercer, M., (2002), *21st Century Goth,* London: Reynolds & Hearn

[142] Udo, T., (2002), *Nine Inch Nails,* London: Sanctuary Publishing

[143] Hodkinson, P., (2002), *Goth: Identity, Style and Subculture,* Oxford: Berg

[144] A term used for old-school Goths, named after the "Batcave" nightclub, opened in London, 1982.

[145] Goodlad, L. M. E., Bibby, M, (2007), *Goth: Undead Subculture,* North Carolina: Duke University Press

[146] Gregory, H., (2010), *Until The Light Takes Us: Interview with the Directors,* [online] Available at: http://www.kqed.org/arts/movies/article.jsp?essid=28163

[147] Kahn-Harris, K., (2000), "'Roots:' The relationship between the local and the global within the extreme metal scene," *Popular Music,* 19, 13-18.

The Norwegian Black Metal Scene was a construct of young, middle-class white males.[148] Sexuality among these males never really contributed to the subculture. Euronymous' homosexual activity (Baddeley: 2008) was more likely to be attributed to blaspheme against the Christian bible than due to any latent homosexuality. This profile gives us another clue as to how the Scene faltered so quickly. Masculine dominated subcultures are presented with immediate difficulty as there is no room for inclusion of femininity. Without both male and female constituents, a subculture cannot carry through generations. Similar to biology, the presence of femininity ensures reproduction.[149] The Gothic scene is not as gender-biased (Goodlad, Bibby: 2010), in fact androgyny is actively sought out and bi-sexuality among participants is encouraged.[150] Due to the Gothic subculture's focus on graceful aesthetics, sensuality and art, there is clearly more concepts for a girl who responds to a general definition of femininity to grasp and become enamoured by.[151] In reality, a lot of the contemporary and successful creativity in the Gothic scene can be attributed to female participants, right from the literary work of Anne Rice through to the band 'Evanescence' who reignited mainstream interest in Goth culture after their success with breakthrough album "Fallen."[152] There was very little to be associated with Norwegian Black Metal that would captivate the imagination of the same individuals.

If we are to assume that the right-wing politics were pivotal to the existence of the Black Metal movement then this offers two theories as to why the movement only existed for a short period. If a youth subculture begins in response to a particular political or social issue, such as the hippy movement of the 1960's embracing "free love" and world peace, then the movement only tends to remain vital for a limited period. If the issue is resolved or falls from favour (the incident at 'Altamont' music festival in 1969, is seen as a key point in the demise of the hippy movement),[153] the youth subculture will tend to be succeeded by others when a previous incarnation loses its impetus, just as the "punk" movement with its nihilism and misconduct (Savage: 1992) took over from the hippy movement. In contrast to this, the Gothic subculture never trapped itself within an issue, but transcended mass society and then expanded into social consciousness with its own structures and folklores and cultural iconography.[154] The other theory being that due to the massive distrust of the right-wing in Norway after the war (see above), that once the stories of the transgressions broke out, fringe fans would not be so eager to increase their membership, thus becoming new converts. A sudden obstacle of this nature would counteract any type of growth within the Scene, plus promoters and venue owners may feel less inclined to give the youth permission to play.

---

[148] Sarelin, M., (2010), "Masculinities within Black Metal: Heteronormativity, Protest Masculinity or Queer?" *The Metal Void: The First Gatherings*, Oxford: The Inter-Disciplinary Press.

[149] LeBlanc, L., (2002), *Pretty in Punk: Girl's gender resistance in a boy's subculture,* New Jersey: Rutgers University Press

[150] Brill, D., (2008), *Goth Culture: Gender, Sexuality and Style,* New York, Macmillan

[151] Hurley, K., (2004), *The Gothic Body: Sexuality, Materialism and Degeneration at the Fin de Siècle,* Cambridge: Cambridge University Press

[152] Fallen, (2003), Wind-up Records

[153] Kirkpatrick, R., (2009), *1969: The Year That Everything Changed,* New York: Skyhorse Publishing

[154] Clendinning, E. A., McAuley, K., (2010), "The Call of Cthulhu: Narrativity of the Cult in Metal," *The Metal Void: The First Gatherings,* Oxford: Inter-Disciplinary Press

Norwegian Black Metal's Legacy

If we fast forward to today, we can count the significant bands that still exist whose roots began in Oslo during that tumultuous creative period. 'Immortal' recently reformed in 2006, after three years of inactivity; 'Emperor' split up in 2001, but reunited between 2006 and 2007 to appear at festivals under the banner: "Live Inferno: A Night of Emperial Wrath." Their lead vocalist Ihsahn continues to release solo efforts to immense critical acclaim. The most notorious group 'Mayhem' last released "Order Ad Chao"[155] in 2007, which was received as a return to form, although they are stylistically unrecognisable from the band that released the controversial: "De Mysteriis Dom Sathanas"[156] in 1994, and have ceased to cause controversy outside of their shows (Campion: 2005). 'Darkthrone' and 'Enslaved' continue to release albums on two-year cycles. 'Gorgoroth' experienced trouble after a legal dispute in which Gaahl and bass player Tom Cato Visnes (aka 'King Ov Hell' ex-bassist with 'Gorgoroth') wanted to leave and take the trademarked name with them. However, Infernus the band's sole founder member won the rights to keep it. Infernus then recruited ex-members and released "Quantos Possunt ad Satanitatem Trahunt."[157] King has recently released an album under the "Ov Hell" name.[158] Various other bands that formed in the wake of the Oslo scene have gained fantastic commercial success, which suggests that without the violent nature of certain antagonists, Black Metal, as abhorrent as it is, can and will sell, with 'Enslaved' winning a Norwegian Grammy[159] (music industry award) for their album "Isa,"[160] it appears that after the ashes of the Scene have blown away, the music-buying public are ready to accept Black Metal as a legitimate musical form.

Following the example set by the sonic output of Norway, smaller subcultures (though without the violence and controversy) have erupted elsewhere. The UK has symphonic Black Metal band 'Cradle of Filth,' who act as the scene leaders in a diverse UK Black Metal scene, which contains not only Satanists but Pagans and a growing number of atheist Black Metal bands; expanding Black Metal beyond its idealistic structure to create something relevant. The USA can now lay claim to 'Wolves in The Throne Room' as international Scene leaders of "Transcendental Black Metal,"[161] a strain of Black Metal that observes the environmental elements of the Oslo Scene and weaves it into their own music. The Transcendental Black Metal Scene also consists of previously mentioned bands 'Alcest' of France, who play an incredibly interesting hybrid of Black Metal and dream-pop, and Eastern Europeans: 'Negura Bunget' from Romania, whose compositions resonate the sounds of their surroundings, by fully utilising their own native instruments.[162] Possibly the most surprising and positive aspect of the Norwegian Black Metal Scene, has been the rise of Black Metal bands from countries with more oppressive authoritarian regimes. Egypt's 'Melechesh' and Israel's 'Orphaned Land' combine both Jewish and Arab influences to create unique music that has played a major part in uniting fans from both sides of civil disputes that have torn their countries apart for time

---

[155] Ordo Ad Chao, (2007), Season of Mist

[156] De Mysteriis Dom Sathanas, (1994), Deathlike Silence Productions

[157] Quantos Possunt ad Satanitatem Trahunt, (2009), Regain Records

[158] The Underworld Regime, (2010), Indie Recordings

[159] Gothique, (2005), "Enslaved wins Norwegian Grammy," Metalunderground.com, [online], available at: http://www.metalunderground.com/news/details.cfm?newsid=12444

[160] Isa, (2004), Candlelight Records

[161] Hunt-Hendrix, H., (2010), "Transcendental Black Metal: A vision of apocalyptic humanism," *Hideous Gnosis: Black Metal Theory Symposium 1*, New York: Createspace

[162] See: OM, (2006), Code666 Records

immemorial,[163] possibly the sole means of giving each side a platform to air views reasonably and constructively, through music.

There is still a healthy scene of Satanic Black Metal bands, although now it operates on an international scale. Currently, a band from Sweden called 'Watain,' are being credited with refining Satanic Black Metal along with another Swedish band 'Shining.' The frontmen of these two groups: Erik Danielsson and Niklas Kvarforth, respectively, are notably the most controversial frontmen of 21st Century Black Metal.[164] Erik, a self-confessed Satanist (in the theistic sense), who famously courted controversy by wearing t-shirts of "NSBM bands" (Nationalist Socialist Black Metal) and expressing Nazi salutes in concert in Germany. When asked by a German magazine, he derided NSBM as a "joke" and that "Black Metal doesn't have anything to do with the world as you know it." He told the journalist that NSBM was a "despaired approach" by people who wished to appear extreme, but were limiting themselves to one way of thinking, and this was not expressive of the "perversion and insanity" of Black Metal.[165] Kvarforth, on the other hand is notorious for his self-harming and developing a heroin addiction just to "see what it was like." He recorded his band's latest album "VII: Född Förlorare"[166] under the effects of the drug.[167] He also maintains that he "tries to show kids that it's cool to cut; but they have to cut deeper." Whether this statement was meant metaphorically or literally, it is difficult to tell. Both Kvarforth and Danielsson have inherited Vikernes' and Aarseth's talent for manipulating the media and prove that even if the epicentre of the Black Metal storm is no longer Oslo, the attitudes are still alive and well.

Chapter Conclusion

It is fair to conclude that Black Metal is far more accepted in the spectrum of heavy music, which has left the 90's Norwegian Black Metal subculture ruptured and fractured as more and more bands who claimed to be "TRVE" have fallen by the way side. A worldwide legion dedicated to the "Blackened Art" have risen and taken the influences of 'Emperor,' 'Mayhem,' etc. and evolved them into something new; which as previously mentioned was an enduring problem with the Oslo Scene. As the individuals involved strived to be more extreme in their portrayal of Satanism and anti-Christianity, the music remained static and ceased to progress artistically. In the case of many genres of music, the earlier proponents are highly regarded as original and revolutionary, and those that follow are scoffed at and named derivative (Wagner: 2010).

In the Black Metal Scene's heyday a Black Metal fan was simply that. In the days of "Scene Wars" between Euronymous' group and the Swedish Death Metal Scene, a member's social status was at risk if one even accepted that Entombed's "Left Hand Path"[168] (a landmark Swedish Death Metal album) interpretation of Satanism was in the same league as that expressed by any work by Mayhem (Kristiansen: 2011). Nowadays, it is far more likely to find someone who appreciates both genres, and makes little attempt to differentiate between the two (Kahn-Harris: 2007). This change

---

[163] Dunn, S., McFayden, S., (2008), Global Metal (7 Countries, 3 Continents, 1 Tribe)

[164] Brown, L., (2011), "Blood Pact: Interview with Erik of Watain and Niklas of Shining," *Terrorizer Magazine*, #207, London: Dark arts Ltd.

[165] "Endres," (2007), "Watain- Intervew," Metal.de, [online] Available at: http://www.metal.de/index.php?option=com_articles&view=article&id=36518

[166] VII: Född förlorare, (2011), Spinefarm Records

[167] Bennett, J., (2011), "Chaos Reigns," *Terrorizer*, #211, London: Dark Arts Ltd.

[168] Left Hand Path, (1990), Earache Records

in the culture of metal was unforeseeable while the Norwegian subculture existed and has been a positive outcome of the fragmentation as malevolent acts between the two factions were commonplace (Moynihan Soderlind: 2003). However, we must conclude that reminiscent of the hippy subculture, the Black Metal subculture was a product of its time, and in a similar fashion to the hippy movement, the attitude and underlying emotion that nourished it to remain vital, began to wane. Although Norway still produces genre-defining bands, the connection of these new bands to the Oslo Scene is tenuous at best. The relatively short period and the static nature in which the second wave of Black Metal existed can be said to have contributed to the genre's out-lasting nature as the blueprints that were fashioned, even then had unlimited potential. Unfortunately, with the protagonists pre-determination with primitivism and using as basic recording equipment as possible (Wagner: 2010), this potential was never fully realised.

Trve: The Norwegian Black Metal Scene: A Subcultural study of Transgression through Music.

fig. 5: Kjetil-Vidar Haraldstad, aka 'Frost' drummer with Satyricon and1349, circa 2009

Chapter V: Conclusion

Throughout this paper I have tried to evaluate the Norwegian Black Metal Subculture expanding beyond the crimes that were committed, as these incidents has been covered countless times. Most of the Black Metallers were perfectly happy to play their music, adorn themselves in black clothes and trade tapes. I have tried to expand beyond this narrow view to the sociological aspect of the Subculture; where such a phenomenon came from, why it happened when it did and why it lasted for such a fleeting period, and finally, why did the youths choose to revolutionise Black Metal instead of playing a different genre. In his work "Swedish Death Metal," Ekeroth surmises that most writers (academics and journalists) who cover subjects like extreme metal will tend to focus their narrative on the offensive nature of the lyrics and imagery (Ekeroth: 2008). This method cheapens and glosses over the music and camaraderie that exemplifies the vast majority of youth subculture participants. I have endeavoured to avoid alluding to more of this tired cliché than I needed to make readers aware of.

We have seen that elements of the socio-democratic "Nordic" model, whereas it was a socially-sound system, it was deeply involved in the disaffection of the Norwegian male youth. Ironically, it also supported their actions in allowing them to play music that was so intensely full of hatred. It has been made quite clear that in a modern democracy, even if the opinions of the right-wing are detestable, then it should be more beneficial to allow them a legitimate means to express their views, due to the frustration that unrepresented groups will eventually feel. This frustration may lead to terrorist acts by these minorities. In turn violent acts by such groups will be over-represented and lead to moral panics forming, tarnishing a youth subculture that essentially wanted to do what almost every teenage boy wants to do; play music, watch horror films and rebel against authority figures.[169]

If we analyse the music, and identify Satan as not just a theistic figure, but a force of evil, then it is hard not to see the influence of Nietzsche,[170] especially his text "The Gay Science." This sense of nihilism, although bleak, offered a connection between the musicians and listeners that felt the power of the church over their everyday lives should be rebelled against and is in essence a political charade. 'Darkthrone's' song "Sacrificing to the God of Doubt" claims "those Christian thieves"[171] are responsible for making people believe that the path to heaven can only be traced by their footsteps. Whereas the band believe that "even the narrow paths lead to Rome" implying that the Church has stole from the livelihoods of the Norwegian community in making them believe that they must behave a certain way, where in actual fact, all paths in life go to the same destination- death. This stands as a pivotal indication of where the views of the non-theistic Satanists lay. Rather than believe in Heaven or Hell, the nihilism shines through, and betrays a devil may care attitude. It can also be interpreted as an attempt to guide mankind away from Christianity, which is far more of a misotheist act than a misanthropic act.[172]

The Norwegian Black Metal Scene defies known definitions of subcultures, gangs and neo-tribes and stands completely alone in history as a short-lived youth group. It is unfair to conclude that the Black Metallers were a violent subculture, as the transgressions could all be attributed to a handful of scene members. All youth subcultures have their violent elements, due to the irrationality of youth in general.[173] Not all youth subcultures however, produce music so independently and for so long, and luminaries like Aarseth should be recognised for this painstaking activity. Unfortunately though, the notorious criminal acts will forever be a part of the subculture's explosion into the public eye, and because of this, the association is unshakeable. Unlike the incidents at Altamont which have largely been forgotten in literature concerning the 1960's pop culture.[174] Therefore, it does make it more difficult to separate the issues in hindsight. The hippy movement had existed for approximately ten years prior to Altamont, and no one was even aware of the Satanic Metal Underground before the suicide of Dead. In conclusion, although the Norwegian Black Metal Subculture has the reputation of violence, which is justified by the church burnings, if not the murders/suicide, there is still a wealth of deeply nihilist and esoteric thought running through the musical output. Besides misgivings about the political structure being excessively right-wing; underneath it all was a group of music-obsessed, horror film aficionados exhibiting youthful rebellion.

---

169 Brownlee, S., Hotinski, R., Pailthorp, B., Ragan, E., Wong, K., (1999), *Inside the teen brain*, U.S. New & Report Archive, [online] Available at: http://www.wac77.com/images/70s_img/inside_teen_brain.pdf
170 Kaufmann, W., (1974), *Nietzsche: Philosopher, Psychologist, Antichrist*, Princeton: Princeton University Press
171 Nagell, G., (2004),"Sacrificing to the God of Doubt," *Sardonic Wrath*, Moonfog Productions
172 Phillips, D. Z., (2005), *The Problem of Evil and The Problem of God*. Minneapolis: Augsburg Fortress
173 Bucholtz, M., (2002), "Youth and Cultural Practice," *Annu. Rev. Anthropol.,* 31, 525-552, [online] Available at: http://www.jstor.org/pss/4132891
174 Schowalter, D., (2009), "Remembering the dangers of rock and roll: Toward a historical narrative of the rock festival," Critical Studies in Media Communication, [online] Available at: http://www.tandfonline.com/doi/abs/10.1080/15295030009388377

Bibliography

Aasdal, P., Ledang, M., (2008), *Once Upon a Time in Norway*, Grenzeless Productions

Abram, C., (2011). *Myths of the Pagan North: the Gods of the Norsemen*, London: Continuum

Aites, A., Ewell, A., (2009) *Until the Light Takes Us,* Variance Films

Alisoglu, S., (2006), "The Cult is Alive- Review," *Blabbermouth.net,* [online] available at:
http://www.roadrunnerrecords.com/blabbermouth.net/showreview.aspx?reviewID=693

Aquino, M., (2009), *Church of Satan: Sixth Edition,* [online] Available at:
http://www.xeper.org/maquino/nm/COS.pdf

Arnopp, J., (1993), "We are but slaves of the one with horns," *Kerrang! Magazine,* No. 463,
27/03/1993

Arter, D., (1999), *Scandinavian Politics Today,* Manchester: Manchester University Press.

Baddeley, G., (2002), *Goth Chic: A Connoisseur's Guide to Dark Culture,* London: Plexus Publishing Ltd

Baddeley, G., (2010), *Lucifer Rising: A Book of Sin, Devil Worship & Rock n' Roll,* 3rd edition, Plexus
Publishing Ltd.: London.

Ball, R. A., Curry, G. D., (1995), "The logic of definition in criminology: Purposes and methods for
defining gangs," *Criminology*, 33, 225-245

BBC News, *Norway Country Profile* [online] Available at:
http://news.bbc.co.uk/1/hi/world/europe/country_profiles/1023276.stm

Bennett, A., (1999), "Subcultures or neo-tribes? Rethinking the relationship between youth, style
and musical taste," *Sociology* Vol. 33 No. 3 August 1999: 599–617

Bennett, J., (2011), "Chaos Reigns," *Terrorizer*, #211, London: Dark Arts Ltd.

Beste, P., (2008), *True Norwegian Black Metal*, London: Vice

Bettez-Halnon, K., (2006), "Heavy Metal Carnival and Dis-Alienation: The Politics of Grotesque
Realism," *Symbolic Interaction*, Vol. 29, 1, pp. 33-48.

Blair, E. M., (1993), "Commercialization of Rap Music Youth *Subculture*." *Journal of Popular Culture*
27.3 21-33

Brown, L., (2011), "Blood Pact: Interview with Erik of Watain and Niklas of Shining," *Terrorizer*
Magazine, #207, London: Dark arts Ltd.

Brownlee, S., Hotinski, R., Pailthorp, B., Ragan, E., Wong, K., (1999), *Inside the teen brain*, U.S. New & Report Archive, [online] Available at:
http://www.wac77.com/images/70s_img/inside_teen_brain.pdf

Bowar, C., (2005), *Interview with Bard G. Eithun*, [online] Available at:
http://heavymetal.about.com/od/interviews/a/faust.htm

Boyesen, H. H., Keary, C. F., (1900), *A History Of Norway: From The Earliest Times,* Whitefish: Kessinger Publishing, LLC

Brill, D., (2008), *Goth Culture: Gender, Sexuality and Style,* New York: Macmillan

Bucholtz, M., (2002), "Youth and Cultural Practice," *Annu. Rev. Anthropol.,* 31, 525-552, [online] Available at: http://www.jstor.org/pss/4132891

Bursik, R. J., Gramsick, H. G., (1993), *Neighbourhoods and Crime: The dimensions of effective community control*, New York: Lexington Books

Campion, C., (2005), "In the Face of Death," *The Observer,* [online] Available at:
http://www.guardian.co.uk/music/2005/feb/20/popandrock4

Chanan, M. (1994) *Musica Practica: The Social Practice of Western Music from Gregorian Chant to Postmodernism,* London: Verso

Christie, I., (2003). *Sound of the Beast: the Complete Headbanging History of Heavy Metal,* New York: HarperCollins Publishers Inc.

Clendinning, E. A., McAuley, K., (2010), "The Call of Cthulhu: Narrativity of the Cult in Metal," *The Metal Void: The First Gatherings,* Oxford: Inter-Disciplinary Press

Cloonan, M. (2002) 'Killing Me Softly With His Song: An Initial Investigation into the Use of Popular Music as a Tool of Oppression', *Popular Music,* 21 (1): 27-40.

Cohen, S., (2002), *Folk Devils & Moral Panics*, 3rd Edition Routledge: New York.

Comstock, G. D., (1992), "Dismantling The Homosexual Panic Defence," *Law & Sexuality Rev. Lesbian and Gay Legal Issues,* 81, 2, [online] Available at:
http://heinonline.org/HOL/LandingPage?collection=journals&handle=hein.journals/lsex2&div=10&id=&page=

Cova, B., (1997), "Community & Consumption: towards a definition of the 'linking value' of products or services," *European Journal of Marketing*, 31, 297-316.

Cova, B., Cova, V., (2001), "Tribal Marketing: The tribalisation of society and its impact on the conduct of marketing," *European Journal of Marketing: Societal Marketing in 2002 & Beyond, Special Issue,* [online] Available at: http://visionarymarketing.com/_repository/wanadoo/cova-tribe-2001.pdf

Cronshaw, A., (2000), "Fjords and Fiddles" *World Music, Vol. 1: Africa, Europe and the Middle East,* pp 211–218. New York: Penguin
Curry, G. D., Decker, S. H., (1998), *Confronting Gangs: Crime and community*, Los Angeles: Roxbury

Dahl, H. F., (1999), *Quisling: A Study in Treachery*. Stanton-Ife, A. M., (trans.). Cambridge: Cambridge University Press

Dasent, Sir G. W., (1859), *Popular Tales From The Norse, (Norske Folkeeventyr)* [online] Available at: http://www.gutenberg.org/catalog/world/readfile?fk_files=1472615

Davisson, J., (2010), "Extreme Politics and Extreme Metal: Strange Bedfellows or Fellow Travellers?" *The Metal Void: The First Gatherings*, Oxford: Inter-Disciplinary Press

Den Norske Kirke, *Medlemskap i Den norske kirke* (meaning: Membership of the church of Norway) [online] Available at: http://www.kirken.no/index.cfm?event=doLink&famId=230

Dome, M., (2007), *Murder Music: Black Metal* [online] Available at: http://www.rockworld.tv/MurderMusicPlayer.html

Dunn, S., (2005) *Metal: A Headbanger's Journey,* clip available online at: http://www.youtube.com/watch?v=oQJqZFUell8

Dunn, S., McFayden, S., (2008), *Global Metal (7 Countries, 3 Continents, 1 Tribe),* Banger Films

Ekeroth, D., (2008), *Swedish Death Metal,* Brooklyn: Bazillion Points

Endres, (2007), "Watain- Intervew," Metal.de, [online] Available at: http://www.metal.de/index.php?option=com_articles&view=article&id=36518

Eriksen, T. H., (2006), "We Have Everything But That's All We Have: Outsourcing the Welfare State," *Verkstad* vol. 6, [online] Available at: http://folk.uio.no/geirthe/Outsourcing.html

Esbensen, F-A., Winfree, L. T., He, N., Taylor, T. J., (2001), "Youth Gangs and Definitional Issues: When is a gang a gang, and why does it matter?" *Crime & Delinquency*, 47, 105 [online] Available at: http://tinyurl.com/gang-definition

Esping-Andersen, G., (1999). *Social Foundations of Postindustrial Economies*. Oxford: Oxford University Press.

Eurobarometer, (2005) "Social Values, Science and Technology," *Eurobarometer*, Brussels: European Commission [online] Available at:
http://ec.europa.eu/public_opinion/archives/ebs/ebs_225_report_en.pdf

Evans, D., (2007), *The History of British Magick After Crowley,* Hidden Publishing.

Flowers, S., (1997), *Lords of the Left Hand Path: A History of Spiritual Dissent*. Runa Raven Press.

Frobenius, N., (2004), *Treori Og Praksis,* (meaning: "Theory and Practice"), Oslo: Gyldendal

Furniss, O., (2010), "Oslo: Norway's music and Festival Paradise," *guardian.co.uk,* [online] Available at: http://www.guardian.co.uk/travel/2010/jan/30/oslo-norway-music-festivals-gigs

Gardner, R. O., (2010), "Introduction: spaces of Musical Interaction: Scenes, subcultures and communities," *Studies in Symbolic Interaction*, 35. 71-77

Goldstein-Gidoni, O., (2003), "Producers of 'Japan' in Israel: *Cultural appropriation* in a non-colonial context." *Ethnos:Journal of Anthropology* 68.3, 365

Goodlad, L. M. E., Bibby, M, (2007), *Goth: Undead Subculture,* North Carolina: Duke University Press

Goodricke-Clarke, N., (2002), *Black Sun: Aryan Cults, Esoteric Nazism and the Politics of Identity,* New York: New York University Press

Gothique, (2005), "Enslaved wins Norwegian Grammy," Metalunderground.com, [online], available at: http://www.metalunderground.com/news/details.cfm?newsid=12444

Gregory, H., (2010), *Until The Light Takes Us: Interview with the Directors,* [online] Available at: http://www.kqed.org/arts/movies/article.jsp?essid=28163

Grimley, D., (2006), *Grieg: Music, Landscape and Norwegian Cultural Identity*, Suffolk: Boydell Press

Gullestad, M., (2002), "Invisible fences, Egalitarianism, Nationalism and Racism," *J. Roy. anthrop. Inst.,* 8, pp. 45-63
        -, (2004), "Blind Slaves of our Prejudices: Debating 'Culture' and 'Race' in Norway," *Ethnos: Journal of Anthropology,* Vol. 69, 2, pp.177-203

Hale, C., (2003), *Himmler's Crusade: The Nazi Expedition to Find the Origins of the Aryan Race,* Hoboken, N.J.: John Wiley & Sons,

Hall, S. Jefferson, T., (1993), Resistance through Rituals: Youth Subcultures in Post-War Britain,London: Routledge

Hayes, P. M., (1971), *Quisling: the career and political ideas of Vidkun Quisling, 1887–1945*, David & Charles: United Kingdom

Hebdige, D., (1979), *Subculture: The Meaning of Style,* New York: Routledge

Hellhammer interviewed by Dmitry Basik (June 1998)

Hoare, J., (2009), "Left Hand Pathfinders". *Terrorizer* #182, London: Dark Arts Ltd.

Hodkinson, P., (2002), *Goth: Identity, Style and Subculture,* Oxford: Berg

Hohler, E. B., (1999). *Norwegian Stave Church Sculpture.* Oslo: Scandinavian University Press

Howell, J. C., (1998), "Youth Gangs: An Overview," *Juvenile Justice Bulletin,* Washington DC: Office of Juvenile Justice and Delinquency Prevention.

Howes, D., (1996), *Cross-cultural consumption: global markets, local realities.* New York: Routledge
http://tinyurl.com/oslo-to-notodden

Huber, E., Stephens, J.D., (2001), *Development & Crisis of the Welfare State: Parties & Policies in Global Markets,* Princeton: Princeton University Press

Hunt-Hendrix, H., (2010), "Transcendental Black Metal: A vision of apocalyptic humanism," *Hideous Gnosis: Black Metal Theory Symposium 1*, New York: Createspace

Huq, R., (2006) *'Beyond subculture'* New York: Routledge

Hurley, K., (2004), *The Gothic Body: Sexuality, Materialism and Degeneration at the Fin de Siècle,* Cambridge: Cambridge University Press

Kahn-Harris, K., (2000), "'Roots:' The relationship between the local and the global within the extreme metal scene," *Popular Music,* 19, 13-18.

    -, (2003), "The Aesthetics of Hate Music," *Institute of Jewish Policy Research,* [online] Available at: http://www.axt.org.uk/HateMusic/KahnHarris.htm

    -, (2004), "The "Failure" of Youth Culture: Reflexivity, Music & Politics in the Black Metal Scene," *European Journal of Cultural Studies,* 7 (1), pp. 95-111. [online] Available at: http://eprints.gold.ac.uk/2196/

    -, (2007), *Extreme Metal: Music and Culture on the Edge,* London: Berg

Kalis, Q., (2004) *Black Metal: A brief guide,* [online] Available at: http://www.chroniclesofchaos.com/Articles/rants/6-668_black_metal_a_brief_guide.aspx

Kaufmann, W., (1974), *Nietzsche: Philosopher, Psychologist, Antichrist,* Princeton: Princeton University Press

Larsen, K., (1948) *A History of Norway,* Princeton: Princeton University Press

Kirkpatrick, R., (2009), *1969: The Year That Everything Changed,* New York: Skyhorse Publishing

Klein, M. W., (1971), *Street Gangs and Street Workers*, New Jersey: Prentice Hall

Kristiansen, J., (1992), "Mayhem," *Slayer Issues 3&4: A Thrash Metal Attack,* Sarpsborg: Self-published

-, (2008), "An Introduction to True Norwegian Black Metal" *True Norwegian Black Metal,* London: Vice

-, (2011), "Metalion: The Slayer Mag. Diaries" New York: Bazillion Points

Kunhemund, G., (2008), "GORGOROTH Frontman Opens Up About His Sexual Orientation: 'I've Never Made Any Secret About It' - Oct. 29, 2008" *RockHard (Ger.) via Blabbermouth.net.* [online] Available at:
http://www.roadrunnerrecords.com/blabbermouth.net/news.aspx?mode=Article&newsitemID=107
859

Kupperman, J. S., (2001) "A History of the Western Mystery Tradition to the Twentieth Century: The Mythology of Magic," *Journal of The Western Mystery Tradition*, Vol. 0, [online] Available at:
http://www.jwmt.org/v1n0/history.html

LeBlanc, L., (2002), *Pretty in Punk: Girl's gender resistance in a boy's subculture,* New Jersey: Rutgers University Press

Longfellow, H. W., (1863), "The Saga of King of Olaf," *Tales of a Wayside Inn: Part First, The Musician's Tale.* [online] Available at: http://www.gutenberg.org/ebooks/25153

Maffesoli, M., (1996), *The Time of the Tribes: The Decline of Individualism in Mass Society,* London: Sage

Mercer, M., (2002), *21st Century Goth,* London: Reynolds & Hearn

Minton, J., (2010), "Interview with Varg Vikernes," *Terrorizer* #194, March, London: Dark Arts Ltd.

Mirosa, M., (2005), *Neo-Tribal Consumption of Ideologies: Insights from new social movement theory,* University of Otago, [online] Available at:
http://otago.academia.edu/MirandaMirosa/Papers/367078/Neo-
Tribal_Consumption_of_Ideologies_Insights_From_New_Social_Movement_Theory

Mitchell, C., (2005), "Interview with Varg Vikernes (10.05.2005),"*Metalcrypt E-zine,* [online] available at: http://www.burzum.org/eng/library/2005_interview_metalcrypt.shtml

Moynihan, M., Soderlind, D., (2003), *Lords of Chaos*, 2nd Edition, Washington: Feral House

Mudrian, A., (2004), *Choosing Death: The Improbable History of Death Metal and Grindcore*, Washington: Feral House.

Myers, B., (2009), "Don't blame black metal for Varg Vikernes' extremism," *The Guardian*, [online] Available at: http://www.guardian.co.uk/music/musicblog/2009/mar/12/varg-vikernes-grishnackh-black-metal?INTCMP=SRCH

Overell, R., (2010), "Brutal belonging in Melbourne's Grindcore Scene," *Studies in Symbolic Interaction,* 35, 79-99

Page, R. I. (1999), *An Introduction to English Runes,* Boydell Press,

        -, (2005), *Runes*, pp. 8, 15, and 16, The British Museum Press.

Patterson, M., (1998) "Direct marketing in postmodernity: neo-tribes and direct communications", *Marketing Intelligence & Planning*, Vol. 16, 1, pp.68 - 74

Perdue, D., Durrschmidt, J., Jowers, P., Doherty, R., (1997), "DIY culture and extended milieux: LETS, veggie boxes and festivals," *The Sociological Review,* 431-441

Phillips, D. Z., (2005), *The Problem of Evil and The Problem of God*. Minneapolis: Augsburg Fortress

Polish Holocaust Magazine, (1995) "Interview with Gaahl" Available at: http://i355.photobucket.com/albums/r455/WD37/76ec8a07.jpg

Putnam, R. D., (2008), E Pluribus Unum: Diversity and Community in the 21st Century," *Scandinavian Political Studies*, 30, 2, 137-174

Rokken, S., Valen, H., (1962), "The Mobilization of the Periphery: Data on Turnout, Party Membership and Candidate Recruitment in Norway," *Acta Sociologica*, Vol. 6, 1, 111-152.

Sampar, M., (2005), "Rock n Roll Suicide: Why Heavy Metal musicians cannot be blamed for the violent acts of their listeners," Seton Hall Journal of Sports and Entertainment Law, 15, 173-196.

Sanchez, R. C., (1992), "Dead & Buried: Mayhem" *Terrorizer Magazine: Black Metal Special #128,* Dark Arts Ltd: London.

Sarelin, M., (2010), "Masculinities within Black Metal: Heteronormativity, Protest Masculinity or Queer?" *The Metal Void: The First Gatherings*, Oxford: The Inter-Disciplinary Press

Savage, J., (1992), *England's Dreaming: Anarchy, Sex Pistols, Punk Rock and Beyond*, London: St. Martin's Press

Schowalter, D., (2009), "Remembering the dangers of rock and roll: Toward a historical narrative of the rock festival," Critical Studies in Media Communication, [online] Available at: http://www.tandfonline.com/doi/abs/10.1080/15295030009388377

Schwarz, P., (2000), *Foreseeing the Future of Music,* [online] Available at: http://www.chroniclesofchaos.com/articles/chats/1-291_earache_records.aspx

Shakespeare, S., (2010), "The Light That Illuminates Itself, the dark that soils itself: Blackened notes from Schelling's Underground," *Hideous Gnosis: Black Metal Theory Symposium I,* New York: Createspace

Soucy, D. & Volkmar, M, (2006), *True Mayhem in Norway,* [online] Available at: http://www.nmchs.com/activities/talon/tal06nov/p07novtal.pdf

Spracklen, K., (2010), "True Aryan Black Metal: The Meaning of Leisure, Belonging and Construction of Whiteness in Black Metal Music," *The Metal Void: First Gatherings,* Inter-Disciplinary Press

Statistics Norway,(n.d.) [online] Available at: http://www.ssb.no/english/subjects/02/befolkning_en/

Steinke, D., (1996), "Satan's Cheerleaders," *SPIN Magazine,* February, pg.62-71

Stortinget, *Constitution- Complete Text,* [online] Available at: http://www.stortinget.no/en/In-English/About-the-Storting/The-Constitution/The-Constitution/

Suffredini, K. S., (2001), "Pride & Prejudice: The Homosexual Panic Defence" *Third World L. J.,* 21, 279, [online] Available at: http://heinonline.org/HOL/LandingPage?collection=journals&handle=hein.journals/bctw21&div=13&id=&page=

SWF Institute, *Sovereign Wealth Fund Rankings: Largest Sovereign Wealth Funds by Assets Under Management,* [online] Available at: http://www.swfinstitute.org/fund-rankings/

Taylor, L. W., (2010), "Nordic Nationalisms: Black Metal takes Norway's Everyday Racism to the Extreme" *The Metal Void: the First Gatherings,* Oxford: Inter-Disciplinary Press
Thornton, S., (1995), *Club Cultures: Music, Media, and Subcultural Capital.* Cambridge: Polity Press.

Thrasher, F. M., (1927) The Gang: A Study of 1313 gangs in Chicago, Chicago: Chicago University Press

Torstein, G., (1998), *Satan Rides The Media (Satan rir Media),* self-published

Udo, T., (2002), *Nine Inch Nails,* London: Sanctuary Publishing

Vikernes, V., (2004), "Part II: Euronymous," *A Burzum Story,* www.burzum.org

Von Billerbeck, L. L., Nordhausen, F., (2001) *Satanskinder, Der Mordfall von Sondershausen und die rechte Szene*. 3. revised edition, Berlin

Von Helden, I., (2011), "'A Forure Normannorum, Libera Nos Domine!' *A Short History of Going Berserk in Scandinavian Literature & Heavy Metal,"* Can I Play With Madness?*, Oxford: Inter-Disciplinary Press

Wagner, J., (2010), *Mean Deviation: Four Decades of Progressive Heavy Metal*, Brooklyn: Bazillion Points.

Wright, J., (2005), *God's Soldiers: Adventure, Politics, Intrigue and Power- A History of the Jesuits*, New York: Image

Yinger, J. M., (1960), "Contraculture and Subculture," *American Sociological Review*, vol. 25, 5.

Appendix

Appendix. I: Election Results of Norwegian General Elections, 1985, 1989, 1993

September 9, 1985 General Election Results - Norway Totals

Registered Electors	3,100,479	
Total Votes	2,605,436	84.00%
Rejected Votes	3,619	0.10%
Valid Votes	2,601,817	99.90%

List	Votes	%	Seats
Norwegian Labour Party	1,061,712	40.8	71
Conservative Party (Høyre)	791,537	30.4	50
Christian Democratic Party (Kristelig Folkeparti)	214,969	8.3	16
Center Party	171,770	6.6	12
Socialist Left Party	141,950	5.5	6
Progress Party	96,797	3.7	2
Liberal Party (Venstre)	81,202	3.1	0
Red Electoral Alliance	14,818	0.6	0
Others	27,062	1	0

September 11, 1989 General Election Results - Norway Totals

Registered Electors	3,190,311	
Total Votes	2,653,173	83.20%
Rejected Votes	5,569	0.20%
Valid Votes	2,647,604	99.80%

List	Votes	%	Seats
Norwegian Labour Party	907,393	34.3	63
Conservative Party (Høyre)	588,682	22.2	37
Progress Party	345,185	13	22
Socialist Left Party	266,782	10.1	17
Christian Democratic Party (Kristelig Folkeparti)	224,852	8.5	14
Center Party	171,269	6.5	11
Future for Finnmark	8,817	0.3	1
Liberal Party (Venstre)	84,740	3.2	0
Environment and Solidarity	22,139	0.8	0
Others	27,745	1	0

September 13, 1993 General Election Results - Norway Totals

Registered Electors	3,259,957	
Total Votes	2,472,551	75.80%
Rejected Votes	10,602	0.40%
Valid Votes	2,461,949	99.60%

List	Votes	%	Seats
Norwegian Labour Party	908,724	36.9	67
Center Party	412,187	16.7	32
Conservative Party (Høyre)	419,373	17	28
Socialist Left Party	194,633	7.9	13
Christian Democratic Party (Kristelig Folkeparti)	193,885	7.9	13
Progress Party	154,497	6.3	10
Liberal Party (Venstre)	88,985	3.6	1
Red Electoral Alliance	26,360	1.1	1
Others	63,305	2.6	0

Appendix. II: Church of Satan- Satanic Rites & Beliefs by LaVey, Anton Szandor

The Nine Satanic Statements

The Nine Satanic Statements outline what "Satan" represents in the Church of Satan

1. Satan represents indulgence instead of abstinence.
2. Satan represents vital existence instead of spiritual pipe dreams.
3. Satan represents undefiled wisdom instead of hypocritical self-deceit.
4. Satan represents kindness to those who deserve it instead of love wasted on ingrates.
5. Satan represents vengeance instead of turning the other cheek.
6. Satan represents responsibility to the responsible instead of concern for psychic vampires.
7. Satan represents man as just another animal, sometimes better, more often worse than those that walk on all-fours, who, because of his "divine spiritual and intellectual development", has become the most vicious animal of all.
8. Satan represents all of the so-called sins, as they all lead to physical, mental, or emotional gratification.
9. Satan has been the best friend the Church has ever had, as He has kept it in business all these years.

The Nine Satanic Sins

1. Stupidity
2. Pretentiousness
3. Solipsism
4. Self-deceit
5. Herd Conformity
6. Lack of Perspective
7. Forgetfulness of Past Orthodoxies
8. Counterproductive Pride
9. Lack of Aesthetics

The Eleven Satanic Rules of the Earth

1. Do not give opinions or advice unless you are asked.
2. Do not tell your troubles to others unless you are sure they want to hear them.
3. When in another's lair, show them respect or else do not go there.
4. If a guest in your lair annoys you, treat them cruelly and without mercy.
5. Do not make sexual advances unless you are given the mating signal.
6. Do not take that which does not belong to you unless it is a burden to the other person and they cry out to be relieved.
7. Acknowledge the power of magic if you have employed it successfully to obtain your desires. If you deny the power of magic after having called upon it with success, you will lose all you have obtained.
8. Do not complain about anything to which you need not subject yourself.
9. Do not harm little children.
10. Do not kill non-human animals unless you are attacked or for your food.
11. When walking in open territory, bother no one. If someone bothers you, ask them to stop. If they don't stop, destroy them.

Appendix. III Discography

The following is a discography of the albums that have been researched pertaining to this paper, including other albums that were important to comprehending Black Metal.

Works Cited:

Burzum, (1993), *Aske,* Deathlike Silence Productions.
     -, (1997), *Dauði Baldrs,* Misanthropy Records
     -, (1999), *Hliðskjálf,* Misanthropy Records
     -, (2010), *Belus,* Byelobog Productions

Darkthrone, (2004), *Sardonic Wrath,* Moonfog Productions
     -, (2006), *The Cult Is Alive,* Peaceville Records
     -, (2008), *Dark Thrones & Black Flags*, Peaceville Records.

Enslaved, (2004), *Isa,* Candlelight Records

Entombed, (1990), *Left Hand Path,* Earache Records

Evanescence, (2003), *Fallen,* Wind-up Records

Gorgoroth (2006), *Ad Majorem Sathanas Gloriam*, Regain Records
     -, (2009), *Quantos Possunt ad Satanitatem Trahunt,* Regain Records

Mayhem, (1994), *De Mysteriis Dom Sathanas,* Deathlike Silence Productions
     -, (2007), *Ordo Ad Chao,* Season of Mist

Negură Bunget, (2006), *Om,* Code666 Records

Ov Hell, (2010), *The Underworld Regime,* Indie Recordings

Shining, (2011*), VII: Född förlorare*, Spinefarm Records

Venom, (1982), Black Metal, Neat Records

Other important Albums:

Aalloch, (2010), *Marrow of the Spirit,* Profound Lore Records

Alcest, (2010), *Écailles de Lune,* Prophecy Productions

Darkthrone, (1992), *A Blaze in the Northern Sky,* Peaceville Records
     -, (1994), *Transilvanian Hunger,* Peaceville Records

Emperor, (1994), *In The Nightside Eclipse,* Candlelight Records

Gorgoroth, (1997), *Under The Sign of Hell,* Malicious Records

Mayhem, (1986), *Pure F**king Armageddon,* Demo
    -, (1987), Deathcrush, Posercorpse Records
    -, (1995), *Dawn of the Black Hearts,* (bootleg), Warmaster Records
    -, (2000), *Grand Declaration of War,* Season of Mist

Wolves in the Throne Room, (2006), *Diadem of 12 Stars,* Southern Lord Recordings

www.ingramcontent.com/pod-product-compliance
Lightning Source LLC
Chambersburg PA
CBHW070828260726
48654CB00024B/570